FLORIDA

DRIVER'S

PRACTICE TESTS

+ 360 DRIVING TEST QUESTIONS TO HELP
YOU ACE YOUR DMV EXAM.

**THE
DRIVING
SCHOOL**

CONTENT

INTRODUCTION

First of all, thank you for choosing this book. As you work through it, you'll find a variety of questions to help you prepare for the DMV test. The questions are based on the information in the Driver's Manual of your state and each one is designed to help you better understand the material.

The best way to use the questions in this book is by practicing them. You can do that by following these steps:

- Take a diagnostic test so you may quickly detect gaps in your driving knowledge and obtain a rough estimate of how much you know about driving rules.
- Take the practice tests from beginning to end without stopping.
- After you have finished, review all of your incorrect answers and read the explanations provided, in the answer key, in the back of this book.
- Join the Facebook group and share questions or doubts with other students.

Remember, the more you practice, the better you'll perform on the real DMV exam.

In order to help you practice for your DMV test, each question has an answer and a corresponding explanation. In some cases, more than one answer might seem correct. In these cases, there will be explanations, after all of the possible responses, to help you understand why those answers are wrong and the other one is correct.

The Florida Driver's Handbook

The Florida Department of Motor Vehicles recommends that you study the official manual. Please read it at least once to get a feel of what you will need to know to pass your exam.

Scan the QR code or type the link in your browser to download it.

https://www.flhsmv.gov/resources/handbooks-manuals/

Cheat Sheets

Don't forget to download your Cheat Sheets, which will tremendously assist you in reviewing the top 100 questions on the DMV written test. Definitely worth reading before your exam. You will find them at the end of the book before the Answer Sheets.

We wish you the best of luck and encourage you to take our practice tests as many times as possible!

So don't wait any longer. Start studying today and you'll be ready to ace your DMV exam! Thanks again for choosing this book. We hope it helps you achieve your driving goals.

And don't forget to write a review of the book. We'd love to hear from you.

About us - The Driving School

We provide education services to people who want to learn how to drive. The company's mission is 'to provide safe and competent drivers for our streets and highways'. We achieve this mission by helping people pass their DMV written exams.

JOIN OUR FACEBOOK GROUP

Share your experience with other students and get answers to questions you might have! Scan the QR code below or type the link into your browser to join.

QR CODE

LINK TO THE GROUP

https://www.facebook.com/groups/953090518945188/

DIAGNOSTIC TEST

Are you just getting started with your study plan and don't know where to begin? With this DMV Diagnostic Test, you may quickly detect gaps in your driving knowledge and obtain a rough estimate of how much you know about driving rules.

Total Questions 15
Correct Answer to pass 12

Question 1 - Diagnostic Test

If you are convicted of reckless driving, you will obtain_____ points on your driving record.

- ☐ 6
- ☐ 4
- ☐ 5
- ☐ 3

Question 2 - Diagnostic Test

You've arrived at an intersection to take a left on a green arrow signal. The arrow indication then turns yellow. So, what should you do now?

- ☐ Take a left
- ☐ Stop
- ☐ Make a 180-degree turn
- ☐ Slow down your vehicle

Question 3 - Diagnostic Test

This symbol denotes

☐   a roadblock in a construction zone

☐   an interstate highway guide sign

☐   a caution sign in a construction zone

☐   an object marker on a roadside

Question 4 - Diagnostic Test

If you are guilty of passing a stopped school bus with its red lights flashing, _____ points will be added to your driving record

☐   5

☐   6

☐   4

☐   2

Question 5 - Diagnostic Test

What is the significance of this flashing arrow panel?

☐   The lane ahead has been closed

☐   The lane ahead of you is open for traffic

☐   The left lane curves ahead

☐   Flaggers (those who wave flags) are in front

Question 6 - Diagnostic Test

What exactly does this sign mean?

☐   You are not permitted to park to the left of the sign

☐   You are not permitted to park on either side of the sign

☐   You can park on the left side of the sign at night

☐   Parking is available to the left of the sign

Question 7 - Diagnostic Test

You may ride your bicycle on a one-way street with two or more traffic lanes under which condition?

☐   (a) on the left side of the street

☐   (b) along the roadway's right edge

☐   (a) or (b)

☐   (c) in the middle of the roadway

Question 8 - Diagnostic Test

When do you have the authority to pass on the right?

☐   On a hill or curve with poor vision ahead

☐   When a vehicle makes or is ready to make a right turn

☐   When a vehicle makes or is about to make a left turn

☐   In none of the preceding scenarios

Question 9 - Diagnostic Test

What exactly does this road sign mean?

☐   A construction zone is ahead

☐   Parking area ahead

☐   The forest zone is ahead

☐   There's a rest area ahead

Question 10 - Diagnostic Test

This sign indicates

☐   the road ahead bends to the right, then to the left

☐   a winding path

☐   the road ahead takes a right turn

☐   there will be severe right and left twists ahead

Question 11 - Diagnostic Test

A _____denotes the outer border of a roadway and may only be crossed by traffic traveling to or from the shoulder.

- ☐ single solid white line
- ☐ shattered white line
- ☐ shattered yellow line
- ☐ single solid yellow line

Question 12 - Diagnostic Test

This symbol indicates

- ☐ there is a right turn ahead
- ☐ there is a double curve ahead
- ☐ a winding journey lies ahead
- ☐ there is a right-hand curve ahead

Question 13 - Diagnostic Test

A constant red arrow pointing right denotes

- ☐ you may turn in the direction indicated by the arrow
- ☐ you must come to a halt and cannot go in the direction of the arrow
- ☐ before making a turn, you must come to a complete stop and yield to oncoming traffic
- ☐ before making a turn, you must slow down and yield to oncoming traffic

Question 14 - Diagnostic Test

What exactly does this sign mean?

☐ Vehicles are not permitted to make a U-turn at the sign

☐ U-turns are not permitted for trucks

☐ At the sign, all vehicles must make a U-turn

☐ It denotes none of the above

Question 15 - Diagnostic Test

This symbol is

☐ a roadside exit sign

☐ a sign indicating the destination's distance

☐ a sign indicating a highway interchange

☐ a sign indicating a destination direction

PRACTICE TEST 1

Get prepared for the DMV driving permit test exam by practicing with real questions that are very similar (often identical!) to those on the DMV test.

Total Questions: 40
Correct Answer to pass: 33

Question 1 - Practice Test 1

Yellow lines are used on one-way streets as

- ☐ lines on the right
- ☐ lines in the middle
- ☐ left-edge lines

Question 2 - Practice Test 1

What should you do to recover from hydroplaning?

- ☐ Hit the brakes
- ☐ Increase the amount of force you apply to the accelerator
- ☐ Firmly hit the brakes
- ☐ Take your foot off the gas pedal

Question 3 - Practice Test 1

When approaching and entering an acceleration lane, _____ to match the speed of vehicles in through lanes.

- ☐ Accelerate your pace
- ☐ Abruptly reduce your speed
- ☐ Gradually reduce your speed
- ☐ Alter your lane and accelerate

Question 4 - Practice Test 1

To get from a private road to a public road,

☐   you must first activate your four-way flashers

☐   perform a quick turn and enter the roadway, while blowing the horn

☐   you are not required to signal when entering the roadway

☐   you must come to a complete stop and yield to the vehicles on the road

Question 5 - Practice Test 1

In the event of a crash, your _____ protects your head and chest from colliding with the dashboard or windshield.

☐   head restraints

☐   lap belts

☐   shoulder belts

☐   steering wheel

Question 6 - Practice Test 1

Use your _____ when driving in fog, rain or snow.

☐   headlights with low-beams

☐   lights for parking

☐   four-way flashing lights

☐   high-intensity headlights

Question 7 - Practice Test 1

You may pass another vehicle on the right in which of the following situations?

☐   When the vehicle is preparing to make or is making a left turn

☐   When the vehicle is ready to make or is making a right turn

☐   When the vehicle is attempting to make a lane change

☐   None of the above options

Question 8 - Practice Test 1

In road accidents, 40% of fatalities are caused by a collision with the windshield, windshield frame or instrument panel. The majority of these deaths can be avoided by wearing:

☐   a windshield coating

☐   a waist belt

☐   safety goggles

☐   a shoulder belt

Question 9 - Practice Test 1

If you miss a freeway exit, you should

☐   stop and ask for assistance

☐   return to the exit by making a U-turn

☐   return to the exit by backing up

☐   proceed to the next exit

Question 10 - Practice Test 1

When two cars enter an uncontrolled intersection (one not controlled by signs or signals) from different highways at roughly the same time, the vehicle _____ has the right-of-way.

- ☐ on the right
- ☐ on the left
- ☐ signaling first
- ☐ with more passengers

Question 11 - Practice Test 1

If you notice an old person crossing a street, you should

- ☐ stop the person by blowing your horn
- ☐ yield the right-of-way by coming to a complete stop
- ☐ quickly cross the intersection by increasing your speed
- ☐ maintain your speed

Question 12 - Practice Test 1

If you see an emergency vehicle approaching with flashing red or blue lights and a siren, you must

- ☐ reduce your speed and take it slowly
- ☐ speed up to get out of the way
- ☐ pull over and come to a complete stop
- ☐ keep going at the same pace

Question 13 - Practice Test 1

If a bicycle on your right arrives at an uncontrolled intersection (one without signs or signals) around the same time as you, you should

☐   request that the bicyclist change lanes.

☐   proceed because you have the right-of-way.

☐   proceed slowly with the bicycle

☐   yield to the bicycle that arrives first

Question 14 - Practice Test 1

The danger zones around trucks and buses, where accidents are more prone to happen, are referred to as

☐   no-zones

☐   zones where no one is allowed to pass

☐   round-zones

☐   empty-zones

Question 15 - Practice Test 1

Tires that are unbalanced or have low tire pressures can cause

☐   reduced stopping distance

☐   tire wear that is accelerated

☐   increased fuel economy

☐   all of the abovementioned

Question 16 - Practice Test 1

As you reach and enter an acceleration lane:

☐ come to a complete stop, before attempting to merge into the motorway

☐ slowly merge into the motorway

☐ reduce your pace to match the speed of traffic in the through lanes

☐ increase your speed to keep up with the traffic in the through lanes

Question 17 - Practice Test 1

If you intend to turn past an intersection, you should

☐ not signal until you have reached the intersection

☐ provide a signal, just before you make the turn

☐ provide a signal, before entering the intersection

☐ not provide any turn signal

Question 18 - Practice Test 1

Except where prohibited, the three-point turn can be used to

☐ switch lanes.

☐ turn around on a narrow street

☐ pass another vehicle on a narrow road

☐ turn to the left

Question 19 - Practice Test 1

You should never share a lane with a motorcycle since

☐ the motorcycle requires the entire lane width

☐ motorcyclists are exempt from traffic laws

☐ you can be misguided by the motorcyclist

☐ motorcycles aren't equipped with turn signals

Question 20 - Practice Test 1

If your wheels stray onto the road's shoulder, you should:

☐ return to the road by increasing your speed

☐ swerve back onto the road, as soon as possible

☐ apply the brakes to bring the car to a complete stop

☐ slow down and keep on the shoulder

Question 21 - Practice Test 1

On a slick, rainy road, you're driving a vehicle without anti-lock brakes (ABS). What is the most effective approach to bring your vehicle to a stop?

☐ Remove your foot from the gas pedal

☐ Pump the brakes

☐ Firmly press the brake pedal

☐ Shift to the neutral position

Question 22 - Practice Test 1

Which is the correct hand signal to indicate a left turn?

☐   Upward-extended hand and arm

☐   Backwards-extended hand and arm

☐   Outwardly extended hand and arm

☐   hand and arm pointing downward

Question 23 - Practice Test 1

Looking ahead, to the sides and behind the car to foresee issues is an aspect of

☐   defensive driving

☐   distracted driving

☐   disciplined driving

☐   aggressive driving

Question 24 - Practice Test 1

Parking places for people with disabilities are indicated by _____ pavement markings.

☐   white

☐   red

☐   yellow

☐   blue

Question 25 - Practice Test 1

If you are stopped at a traffic light and another vehicle is approaching from behind at high speed,

☐ make a quick U-turn

☐ move your vehicle forward

☐ turn your vehicle to the right

☐ turn your vehicle to the left

Question 26 - Practice Test 1

If you have to park on the road, park your car

☐ as close as possible, to the center of the road

☐ as far away as possible, from the yellow line

☐ as far as possible, away from traffic

☐ as far as possible, away from the curb

Question 27 - Practice Test 1

The hand and arm bent at 90 degrees and pointing to the floor indicate the driver's intention to:

☐ make a turn to the left

☐ stop or slow down

☐ go straight ahead.

☐ make a turn to the right

Question 28 - Practice Test 1

Children under which age group should never be allowed to ride in the front seat of a car?

- ☐ 12 years old and under

- ☐ 14 years old and under

- ☐ 16 years old and under

- ☐ 13 years old and under

Question 29 - Practice Test 1

What should you do if you are the first person to arrive at the scene of a collision?

- ☐ Turn off the ignition of any vehicles involved in the collision

- ☐ Inform the local Police

- ☐ Remove your vehicle from the heavily traveled section of the road

- ☐ Carry out all of the preceding steps

Question 30 - Practice Test 1

Which of the following freeway claims are correct?

- ☐ Freeways are built to safely handle high-speed traffic

- ☐ Cross a solid line immediately after entering or before exiting, while using a freeway

- ☐ Deceleration lanes are available on most motorways to aid drivers in departing

- ☐ Smoothly enter a motorway by accelerating on the entry ramp to match the traffic pace

Question 31 - Practice Test 1

Which of the following claims about highway driving is correct?

☐ Faster cars must use the deceleration lane to join the highway

☐ The right lane provides the smoothest traffic flow, when there are three or more lanes, traveling in the same direction.

☐ The left lane should be used by slower vehicles, whereas the right lane should be used by quicker vehicles

☐ The right lane should be used by slower vehicles, while the left lane should be used by faster vehicles

Question 32 - Practice Test 1

Any vehicle's rear wheels will follow a _____, than its front wheels when it turns.

☐ shorter path

☐ longer path

☐ slower path

☐ faster path

Question 33 - Practice Test 1

Car and motorcycle collisions are more likely to happen in

☐ freeways

☐ roundabouts

☐ intersections

☐ one-way roads

Question 34 - Practice Test 1

A pair of white or longitudinal lines that indicate where pedestrians may walk, is known as

- ☐ lines of Suppression
- ☐ crosswalk lines
- ☐ pavement delineation
- ☐ lines for walking

Question 35 - Practice Test 1

In highway and street work zones, flag persons are operating

- ☐ to find out how much alcohol is in a driver's blood
- ☐ to safely stop, slow or direct vehicles through construction zones
- ☐ to slow vehicles down to the posted speed limit
- ☐ to notify the police and insurance companies about incidents

Question 36 - Practice Test 1

If a vehicle in front of you comes to a complete stop for a pedestrian at a crosswalk, you must

- ☐ change lanes rapidly and pass the vehicle
- ☐ not pass the car that has come to a complete halt
- ☐ reduce your speed and drive slowly past the vehicle
- ☐ proceed with caution after warning the pedestrian

Question 37 - Practice Test 1

When slowing down or coming to a complete stop, you must

☐   (a) make a hand signal to alert the driver in front of you.

☐   (b) use the brake-activated signal lights to warn the driver behind you.

☐   carry out either (a) or (b)

☐   carry out both (a) and (b)

Question 38 - Practice Test 1

What should you do to recover from a skid?

☐   Brake instantly and gently steer your vehicle in the opposite direction of where you want it to go

☐   Brake instantly and gently steer your vehicle in the direction you want it to go

☐   Take your foot off the throttle and slowly steer your vehicle in the direction you want it to go

☐   Take your foot off the accelerator and carefully steer your vehicle in the opposite direction of where you want it to travel

Question 39 - Practice Test 1

Which of the three types of intersections is correct?

☐   Diamond, blind and controlled

☐   Controlled, uncontrolled and blind

☐   Diamond, uncontrolled and controlled

☐   Cloverleaf, controlled and uncontrolled

Question 40 - Practice Test 1

All of the maneuvers listed below are correct while changing lanes, EXCEPT

☐ turning the steering wheel, when you turn your head to check for blind spots

☐ inspecting your rear-view and side-view mirrors

☐ removing your eyes from the ahead, for longer than a split second.

☐ looking over your shoulder in the direction you intend to move, whilst checking for blind spots

PRACTICE TEST 2

Get prepared for the DMV driving permit test exam by practicing with real questions that are very similar (often identical!) to those on the DMV test.

Total Questions: 40
Correct Answer to pass: 33

Question 1 - Practice Test 2

A constant red arrow pointing right denotes

- ☐ you may turn in the direction indicated by the arrow
- ☐ before making a turn, you must slow down and yield to oncoming traffic
- ☐ before making a turn, you must come to a complete stop and yield to oncoming traffic
- ☐ you must come to a halt and cannot go in the direction of the arrow

Question 2 - Practice Test 2

You should do the following during your driving skills test:

- ☐ Only signal if there are no people or other cars in the area
- ☐ Keep to the left lane
- ☐ Keep a two-second following distance behind the vehicle in front of you
- ☐ Maintain a firm grip on the steering wheel with both hands

Question 3 - Practice Test 2

If there is a broken yellow line on your side of the center dash stripe,

- ☐   you are not permitted to cross the line
- ☐   you may cross the line to allow other vehicles to pass
- ☐   only if the other side has a broken line may you cross the line
- ☐   none of the preceding apply

Question 4 - Practice Test 2

If you must park on a roadway, you should park

- ☐   as close to the road's center as feasible
- ☐   as far as possible away from the curb
- ☐   as far as possible away from traffic
- ☐   as far as possible away from the yellow line

Question 5 - Practice Test 2

Another vehicle is passing you on the left. You should allow the other vehicle to pass safely and_____

- ☐   shift to the right side of the road
- ☐   accelerate your pace
- ☐   enter the left lane
- ☐   don't increase your pace

Question 6 - Practice Test 2

You're driving down a two-lane road. If a car in front of you stops for a pedestrian, what should you do?

- ☐ Slow down and pass the vehicle slowly
- ☐ Change lanes rapidly and pass the vehicle
- ☐ Inform the stopped car that it must take a detour
- ☐ Do not overtake the stopped vehicle

Question 7 - Practice Test 2

You are at a stop sign, awaiting a right turn. A car approaching from the left has its turn signal activated. So, what should you do now?

- ☐ Turn ahead since the other vehicle is about to turn as well
- ☐ Wait until the other vehicle begins to turn before beginning your turn
- ☐ Turn on your headlights as soon as possible
- ☐ Immediately depress the gas pedal

Question 8 - Practice Test 2

When do you have the authority to pass the right?

- ☐ When a vehicle makes or is about to make a left turn
- ☐ On a climb or curve with poor vision ahead
- ☐ When a vehicle is ready to make a right turn
- ☐ In none of the preceding scenarios

Question 9 - Practice Test 2

At railroad crossings with merely a stop sign, you must halt and then advance only when

- ☐ you assess that there are no schoolchildren present
- ☐ you determine that no train is on its way
- ☐ you determine that there are no incoming pedestrians
- ☐ you should do all of the aforementioned tasks

Question 10 - Practice Test 2

What does this sign mean?

- ☐ You have the option of continuing straight or turning right
- ☐ You must proceed straight
- ☐ You have the option of continuing straight or turning left
- ☐ You must take a right

Question 11 - Practice Test 2

When passing another car on a two-lane road, you should pass

    ☐   neither on the left nor the right side of the car

    ☐   only on the vehicle's right side

    ☐   either on the left or right side of the vehicle

    ☐   only on the vehicle's left side

Question 12 - Practice Test 2

What do you mean by open intersections?

    ☐   Junctions that are not patrolled by a police officer

    ☐   Crossroads where there is no blinking red light

    ☐   Junctions where there is no posted speed limit

    ☐   Intersections without stop signs, yield signs, or traffic lights

Question 13 - Practice Test 2

If a railroad grade crossing lacks warning equipment or merely has a crossbuck sign, you should

    ☐   come to a complete halt within 100 feet of the railroad crossing

    ☐   accelerate and cross the railroad crossing

    ☐   slow down and take your time

    ☐   change gears and continue through the railroad crossing

Question 14 - Practice Test 2

The most likely locations for vehicle and motorcycle collisions are

    ☐   Intersections

    ☐   One-way streets

    ☐   Expressways

    ☐   Roundabouts

Question 15 - Practice Test 2

Regulatory devices inform you

    ☐   to come to a halt, move in a specific direction, or reduce your speed

    ☐   tips to navigate securely or make your journey more enjoyable

    ☐   of potentially dangerous conditions or the possibility of potentially harmful conditions

    ☐   none of the aforementioned

Question 16 - Practice Test 2

What should you do if you see an oncoming vehicle in your lane?

    ☐   Reduce your speed and honk your horn

    ☐   Veer to the right as far as you can safely

    ☐   Turn on your headlights

    ☐   Complete all of the preceding tasks

Question 17 - Practice Test 2

Which of the following headlamp claims is incorrect?

☐ When going behind other vehicles, high lights are used

☐ Low beams are utilized when traveling in cities and while stuck in traffic

☐ When there is no traffic in sight, high lights are employed in open country driving

☐ When driving in fog, rain, or snow, low lights are employed

Question 18 - Practice Test 2

The right lane of an expressway should be kept open for _____

☐ trucks

☐ traffic entering or exiting the expressway

☐ through traffic

☐ passing traffic

Question 19 - Practice Test 2

What does this sign mean?

☐ There is phone service accessible ahead of time

☐ A hospital is on the way

☐ There will be a rest stop ahead

☐ There will be a petrol station ahead

Question 20 - Practice Test 2

The vertical rectangular signage with black characters on a white background are used as

- ☐ regulatory signs
- ☐ destination signs
- ☐ warning signs
- ☐ service signs

Question 21 - Practice Test 2

This symbol indicates

- ☐ there's a flagger ahead
- ☐ a traffic officer is approaching
- ☐ there is a parking lot ahead
- ☐ pedestrians are crossing the street ahead

Question 22 - Practice Test 2

A double solid yellow line in the middle of the road indicates

- ☐ on either side, passing is not permitted
- ☐ all traffic must come to a halt at the line
- ☐ on both sides, passing is permitted
- ☐ traffic can only flow in one direction

Question 23 - Practice Test 2

A triangular orange sign on the back of a vehicle denotes

☐	The car has a top speed of more than 25 miles per hour
☐	The vehicle's top speed is limited to 45 mph
☐	The vehicle's top speed is limited to 25 mph
☐	The vehicle must move at a speed slower than 55 mph

Question 24 - Practice Test 2

You are driving in congested areas. An emergency car with flashing lights is close behind you. So, what should you do now?

☐	Continue to drive in the same lane and allow the emergency vehicle to change lanes
☐	Increase your speed
☐	Stop right away in your lane
☐	Continue to move until you can get out of the way

Question 25 - Practice Test 2

Which of the following documents may a police officer request from you if you are stopped for a traffic violation?

☐	Vehicle registration
☐	Insurance Proof
☐	A driver's license
☐	Everything mentioned above

Question 26 - Practice Test 2

This sign alerts cars that they are approaching a

   ☐   a two-way street

   ☐   a one-way street

   ☐   a divided highway

   ☐   a single-lane bridge

Question 27 - Practice Test 2

You should NOT do this if another driver is tailgating you

   ☐   Extend your following distance

   ☐   Accelerate your pace

   ☐   Decrease your speed

   ☐   Put yourself in the appropriate lane

Question 28 - Practice Test 2

If traffic from another route merges onto the road you're on, what should you do?

   ☐   Because you have the right-of-way, ignore the merging traffic

   ☐   Change lanes right away

   ☐   Sound your horn to alert merging vehicles to your presence

   ☐   Allow the traffic to merge by adjusting your speed and vehicle position

Question 29 - Practice Test 2

When is it permissible to drive on the shoulder in order to pass another car on the right?

- ☐ If the car comes to a halt due to an emergency
- ☐ If the car is making a left turn
- ☐ Never
- ☐ If the car is making a right turn

Question 30 - Practice Test 2

If there is _____next to your lane, you may pass another vehicle

- ☐ a single continuous yellow line
- ☐ a double yellow solid line
- ☐ a broken white line
- ☐ a continuous white line

Question 31 - Practice Test 2

When a traffic signal at a crossing turns green and you are proceeding straight through, you must

- ☐ keep an eye out for automobiles that are turning
- ☐ wait for the next signal and come to a halt
- ☐ drive as swiftly as possible through the intersection
- ☐ check and make sure that there are no more vehicles entering or exiting the intersection

Question 32 - Practice Test 2

If you intend to stop or slow down in an area where others may not expect it, you should _____to warn people behind you.

     ☐   change lanes fast

     ☐   change lanes fast

     ☐   turn on your emergency flashers as soon as possible

     ☐   tap quickly three or four times on the brake pedal

Question 33 - Practice Test 2

If your engine dies while traveling around a bend, you should

     ☐   pull over your vehicle to the right side of the road

     ☐   maintain a firm grip on the steering wheel and keep your vehicle straight

     ☐   take your foot off the gas pedal

     ☐   on the road, try to restart the engine

Question 34 - Practice Test 2

You should do the following to assist avoid a collision:

     ☐   Keep on the left side of the road

     ☐   Maintain a cushion of space

     ☐   Frequently change lanes

     ☐   Closely follow other vehicles

Question 35 - Practice Test 2

If you abruptly lose control of the steering wheel, what should you do?

☐   Remove your foot from the gas pedal

☐   Set the parking brake

☐   Remove your foot from the brake pedal

☐   Change gears

Question 36 - Practice Test 2

If you must enter an interstate highway from an acceleration lane, you should

☐   keep up with other traffic or adhere to posted speed limits

☐   wait for the space to coalesce before proceeding

☐   merge, go faster than the posted speed limit

☐   reduce your speed

Question 37 - Practice Test 2

What exactly does this sign mean?

☐   There is a Y-intersection ahead

☐   There is a yield sign ahead

☐   A youth hostel awaits

☐   There's a side road ahead

Question 38 - Practice Test 2

**If an approaching car is using its high lights, you should look
_____until the vehicle has passed.**

☐   at the vehicle's driver

☐   in the middle of the road

☐   towards the road's right edge

☐   towards the road's left edge

Question 39 - Practice Test 2

**Which vehicle has the right-of-way when two or more vehicles arrive at
a four-way stop at separate times?**

☐   The vehicle that gives the initial indication should
be the first to leave

☐   The first vehicle to come to a halt should be the
first to go

☐   The vehicle that was the last to stop should be the
first to depart

☐   The larger vehicle should be the first to be
eliminated

Question 40 - Practice Test 2

**What should you do if you come to a stop in front of a persistent yellow
traffic light?**

☐   Accelerate to clear the signal before it turns red

☐   Proceed with extreme caution

☐   After yielding to traffic, proceed through

☐   If you can safely stop, do so

ROAD SIGNS

In the United States, road signs are increasingly using symbols rather than words to convey their message. Symbols allow for immediate communication with road users, overcoming language barriers and are fast becoming the industry standard for traffic control equipment around the world.

Every car driver should be familiar with the symbols on traffic signs to ensure the safety and efficiency of our transportation systems.

We've got you covered with more than 150 questions on Road Signs.

Total Questions: 150
Correct Answer to pass: 120

Question 1 - Road Signs

This symbol indicates

- ☐ a railroad crossing
- ☐ work on the road
- ☐ a left turn
- ☐ road maintenance

Question 2 - Road Signs

What is the significance of this flashing arrow panel?

- ☐   The lane ahead has been closed
- ☐   The lane ahead of you is open for traffic
- ☐   Flaggers (people who wave flags) are in front
- ☐   The left lane curves ahead

Question 3 - Road Signs

This symbol indicates

- ☐   the distance between the current exit and the next
- ☐   an interstate highway number
- ☐   a code of exit
- ☐   the speed limit on interstate highways

44

Question 4 - Road Signs

This symbol indicates

☐ vehicles on the left must turn left, while vehicles on the right must continue straight

☐ vehicles on the left must make a left turn and vehicles on the right must make a right turn

☐ vehicles on the left must turn left, while vehicles on the right may either continue straight or turn left

☐ vehicles on the left must turn left, while those on the right must merge with the right lane

Question 5 - Road Signs

This diagram depicts

☐ a crossroads that lies ahead

☐ a two-way road

☐ a one-way road

☐ crossing traffic is ahead.

Question 6 - Road Signs

What does this sign mean?

☐   A divided highway begins ahead of you

☐   There will be one-way traffic ahead

☐   The divided highway comes to an end ahead

☐   Traffic is congealing ahead

Question 7 - Road Signs

What does this sign mean?

☐   When the green arrow is illuminated, left turns are permitted

☐   When the steady green signal is illuminated and there are no oncoming vehicles, left turns are permitted

☐   When the green arrow flashes, no left turns are permitted

☐   Left turns are only permitted when the steady green signal is not illuminated

Question 8 - Road Signs

What does this sign mean?

☐ Traffic in the right lane must merge to the right, while traffic in the second lane must either go straight or merge to the right

☐ The traffic in the right lane must continue straight, while the traffic in the second lane must turn right

☐ Traffic in the right lane must turn right, while traffic in the second lane must either stay straight or turn left

☐ Traffic in the right lane must turn right, while traffic in the second lane must either stay straight or turn right

Question 9 - Road Signs

What exactly does this sign mean?

☐ There is disabled parking ahead

☐ There is a disabled crossing ahead

☐ A hospital is on the way

☐ There is a pedestrian crosswalk ahead

Question 10 - Road Signs

This warning sign informs drivers that

    ☐   there is a single-use path crossing ahead

    ☐   there is a school zone ahead

    ☐   bicyclists must be allowed to use the lane

    ☐   there is a multi-use path crossing ahead

Question 11 - Road Signs

What exactly does this sign mean?

    ☐   There is a tunnel ahead

    ☐   There is a railroad crossing ahead

    ☐   A work zone awaits

    ☐   A crossroads awaits

Question 12 - Road Signs

What does this image represent?

☐   When the road ahead is clear, passing on the left is permitted

☐   Passing on the left is not permitted

☐   Passing is prohibited in both directions

☐   Passing is only permitted during the day

Question 13 - Road Signs

What exactly does this road sign mean?

☐   A construction zone is ahead

☐   A parking area is ahead

☐   The forest zone is ahead

☐   There's a rest stop ahead

Question 14 - Road Signs

What does this figure represent?

- ☐ A child care centre is on the way
- ☐ There is a T-intersection ahead
- ☐ A playground lies ahead
- ☐ There is a school zone ahead.

Question 15 - Road Signs

This symbol is

- ☐ a service sign
- ☐ a route-marking sign
- ☐ a regulatory indication
- ☐ a cautionary note

Question 16 - Road Signs

What does this sign mean?

- ☐ A side street near a railroad crossing
- ☐ A slender bridge
- ☐ A truck service center
- ☐ A pedestrian overpass

Question 17 - Road Signs

This symbol indicates

- ☐ a hospital area
- ☐ wheelchair accessibility is available
- ☐ a parking area for the handicapped
- ☐ a crosswalk for pedestrians

Question 18 - Road Signs

This orange triangular reflective sign represents

☐   a rapidly moving vehicle

☐   a vehicle transporting dangerous materials

☐   a slow-moving vehicle

☐   a large truck

Question 19 - Road Signs

Which of these signs points you in the direction of a hospital?

A B C D

☐   D

☐   B

☐   A

☐   C

Question 20 - Road Signs

What does this sign mean?

☐ Vehicles are merging ahead, do not accelerate to 45 mph

☐ Drive at a 45-mph speed

☐ A speed zone is ahead, prepare to slow down to 45 mph

☐ Construction ahead, slow down to 45 mph.

Question 21 - Road Signs

Typically, a vertical, rectangular traffic sign provides

☐ guidelines to the driver

☐ directions to the driver to come to a halt

☐ a road number

☐ a warning about the road's condition

Question 22 - Road Signs

This symbol indicates

- ☐   a lane for turning right
- ☐   a diversion
- ☐   the road ahead curves to the left.
- ☐   a lane for turning left

Question 23 - Road Signs

This symbol indicates that

- ☐   bicyclists should only ride in the lane designated by the sign
- ☐   a bikeway crosses the road ahead
- ☐   bicyclists are not permitted to use this lane
- ☐   there is a no-passing zone for bicyclists ahead

Question 24 - Road Signs

If you see this sign while driving in the left lane, what should you do?

- ☐ Continue straight
- ☐ Merge into the right lane
- ☐ Take a left
- ☐ Take a right

Question 25 - Road Signs

This is a warning sign denoting

- ☐ there will be sharp right and left turns ahead
- ☐ the road ahead takes a right turn
- ☐ a winding path
- ☐ the road ahead bends to the right, then to the left

Question 26 - Road Signs

What does this signal mean at an intersection?

☐   Pedestrians are not permitted to enter the crosswalk

☐   Drivers must slow down and exercise caution

☐   Pedestrians who are already in the crosswalk may complete their crossing

☐   Pedestrians are permitted to enter the crosswalk

Question 27 - Road Signs

This symbol indicates

☐   there is a hospital ahead

☐   there is a rest stop ahead

☐   a high school awaits

☐   there is a handicapped service area ahead

Question 28 - Road Signs

What does this image represent?

☐ Under no circumstances, are vehicles permitted to cross the broken yellow line

☐ Vehicles are not permitted to pass or turn across the broken yellow line

☐ Vehicles are only permitted to cross the broken yellow line if it is safe to do so

☐ If it is safe to do so, vehicles may cross the broken yellow line, to pass or turn

Question 29 - Road Signs

This symbol indicates

☐ That Exit number 117 is up ahead

☐ the next available exit is 117 miles away

☐ to get onto Route 117, take this exit.

☐ none of the aforementioned.

Question 30 - Road Signs

This sign indicates the location of

☐　　a gas station

☐　　a communication service

☐　　a place to rest

☐　　a camping area

Question 31 - Road Signs

What does this sign mean?

☐　　The divided highway comes to an end ahead

☐　　A divided highway begins ahead of you

☐　　There's an underpass ahead of you

☐　　The right lane is closed ahead

Question 32 - Road Signs

These highway signs are known as

- ☐ dynamic message signs
- ☐ route marker signs
- ☐ crossroads indicators
- ☐ work zone markers

Question 33 - Road Signs

If you see this sign, it means you are

- ☐ moving in the wrong lane
- ☐ driving in the wrong direction
- ☐ in the city
- ☐ on the highway

Question 34 - Road Signs

What exactly does this sign mean?

- ☐   At night, take Route 45
- ☐   The top speed is 45 miles per hour.
- ☐   The minimum speed limit is 45 miles per hour
- ☐   At night, the maximum speed limit is 45 mph

Question 35 - Road Signs

What exactly does this sign mean?

- ☐   There is a possibility that emergency vehicles will enter the roadway
- ☐   Trucks transporting dangerous materials may enter the road
- ☐   Heavy vehicles may enter the road
- ☐   Farm vehicles have the potential to enter the roadway

Question 36 - Road Signs

What should you do if you come across this sign at an intersection?

- ☐ Do not go any further
- ☐ Continue to the right
- ☐ Allow oncoming traffic to pass
- ☐ Before turning right or left, yield the right-of-way or come to a complete stop

Question 37 - Road Signs

This sign and the pavement markings permits

- ☐ vehicles approaching from either direction to make a right turn
- ☐ vehicles from either direction are permitted to pass
- ☐ vehicles approaching from either direction to make a left turn
- ☐ none of the aforementioned.

Question 38 - Road Signs

What exactly does this sign mean?

☐   At the sign, all vehicles must make a U-turn

☐   U-turns are not permitted for trucks

☐   Vehicles are not permitted to make a U-turn at the sign

☐   It denotes none of the preceding

Question 39 - Road Signs

What exactly does this sign mean?

☐   A side road is ahead, keep an eye out for vehicles entering the road

☐   There will be a T-intersection ahead, yield to cross traffic

☐   There will be a four-way stop ahead, prepare to yield

☐   A tourist information center is ahead, make a stop if necessary

Question 40 - Road Signs

What does this sign mean?

☐   There's a speed limit ahead

☐   On-ramp speed restriction

☐   Speed advisory at the roundabout

☐   Exit speed restriction

Question 41 - Road Signs

What exactly does this sign mean?

☐   Only right turns are permitted

☐   Traffic must merge to the right

☐   Traffic must merge to the left

☐   Only left turns are permitted

Question 42 - Road Signs

What exactly does this sign mean?

- ☐ You must not take a right turn
- ☐ You must not turn left
- ☐ This section of the road is currently closed
- ☐ Do not combine

Question 43 - Road Signs

What exactly does this sign mean?

- ☐ A hospital is on the way
- ☐ There is a telephone service available ahead
- ☐ There will be a gas station ahead
- ☐ There will be a rest stop ahead

Question 44 - Road Signs

What exactly does this sign mean?

☐　　　You're about to approach a left turn

☐　　　You're about to approach a right turn

☐　　　A sharp U-turn is on the way

☐　　　A sharp left turn awaits

Question 45 - Road Signs

What should you do if you see this road sign?

☐　　　Exit the highway at a minimum speed of 30 miles per hour

☐　　　Exit the highway at a speed of 30 miles per hour or less

☐　　　Pass the vehicle in front of you by increasing your speed to 30 mph

☐　　　With a top speed of 60 mph, exit the highway

Question 46 - Road Signs

This image's pavement markings indicate that

- ☐ it is not permitted to pass
- ☐ it is permissible to pass
- ☐ drivers are required to take a detour
- ☐ drivers must make a turn

Question 47 - Road Signs

What is the nature of this sign?

- ☐ A sign saying 'Do Not Enter'
- ☐ A yield sign
- ☐ A stop sign
- ☐ A one-way street sign

Question 48 - Road Signs

What does this traffic sign mean?

☐   Passing a vehicle on the left is not permitted

☐   Only left turns are permitted

☐   In these directions, passing is permitted

☐   Only move in the directions indicated

Question 49 - Road Signs

What exactly does this sign mean?

☐   A hospital is near

☐   Approaching a four-way intersection

☐   There's a side road ahead

☐   There is a railroad crossing ahead

Question 50 - Road Signs

What exactly does this sign mean?

- ☐   Large trucks are not permitted on this road

- ☐   Trucks are not permitted to park here

- ☐   On this road, only large trucks are permitted

- ☐   On this road, only high-occupancy vehicles (HOVs) are permitted

Question 51 - Road Signs

This symbol indicates

- ☐   a railroad crossing with low ground clearance

- ☐   a railroad crossing that is closed

- ☐   a railroad crossing that is being repaired

- ☐   a byway near a railroad crossing

Question 52 - Road Signs

What does this image represent?

☐   A shattered white line that forbids passing

☐   A broken white line that permits passing

☐   An accident occurred as a result of a shorter following distance.

☐   A vehicle making a U-turn

Question 53 - Road Signs

This is an octagonal (eight-sided) figure which means

☐   a yield symbol

☐   a sign that says 'Do Not Enter'

☐   a stop sign

☐   a construction sign on a road

Question 54 - Road Signs

This orange sign can be found at

- ☐ crossings of railroads
- ☐ intersections that are uncontrolled
- ☐ zones around schools
- ☐ work zones

Question 55 - Road Signs

This symbol can be used to

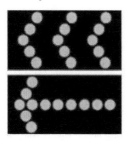

- ☐ direct drivers into specific traffic lanes
- ☐ direct drivers to perform a U-turn
- ☐ warn drivers that there is a one-way street ahead
- ☐ make drivers aware of the presence of a school zone

Question 56 - Road Signs

This sign informs the driver that the road is a

☐   a winding road

☐   a double curve

☐   the road is slick.

☐   a two-way street

Question 57 - Road Signs

This sign expresses concern that

☐   a winding road awaits, drivers should follow the signs

☐   there is a gravel road ahead with sharp curves, drivers must proceed with caution

☐   when the road is wet, it becomes slick and drivers must proceed cautiously

☐   there is a sharp curve near a hill, vehicles must proceed cautiously

Question 58 - Road Signs

This symbol is a

- ☐   sign that says 'Right Lane Ends'

- ☐   sign for a freeway interchange

- ☐   sharp turn on a highway

- ☐   beginning of a Divided Highway sign

Question 59 - Road Signs

This diamond-shaped symbol denotes

- ☐   there is a median ahead, the road width is 13 feet 6 inches

- ☐   there is a bridge ahead, the road width is 13 feet 6 inches

- ☐   there is an overpass ahead with a clearance of 13 feet 6 inches from the roadway surface to the overpass

- ☐   there is a parking area ahead, the road width is 13 feet 6 inches

Question 60 - Road Signs

What exactly does this sign mean?

- ☐ You are not permitted to park on either side of the sign
- ☐ You can park on the left side of the sign at night
- ☐ Parking is available to the left of the sign
- ☐ You are not permitted to park to the left of the sign

Question 61 - Road Signs

What does this sign mean?

- ☐ A deer is crossing ahead
- ☐ A cattle crossing is ahead
- ☐ The forest zone is ahead
- ☐ There is a zoo ahead

Question 62 - Road Signs

What does this sign mean?

☐ At any time, the maximum permissible speed in a school zone

☐ At any time, the minimum permissible speed in a school zone

☐ When there are children present in a school zone, this is the maximum permissible speed

☐ When there are children present in a school zone, this is the minimum permissible speed

Question 63 - Road Signs

This service sign specifies that

☐ there is parking available

☐ there is lodging available

☐ there is a hospital service available

☐ there is a service area available

Question 64 - Road Signs

What is the significance of this regulatory sign?

☐ During the times specified, the indicated lane is for high-occupancy vehicles

☐ High-occupancy vehicles are not permitted at certain times

☐ During the specified times, no cars or buses are permitted

☐ The designated lane is for large trucks

Question 65 - Road Signs

A stop sign accompanied by this sign at an intersection indicates that

☐ you must come to a complete stop for four seconds.

☐ there are four traffic lanes.

☐ vehicles approaching from all four directions must yield

☐ vehicles approaching the intersection from all four directions must come to a complete stop

Question 66 - Road Signs

What exactly does this sign mean?

- ☐ The road ahead is closed
- ☐ This road comes to an end at a T-intersection
- ☐ A narrow bridge's rails are ahead
- ☐ There will be a Y-intersection ahead

Question 67 - Road Signs

This symbol indicates

- ☐ to enter Route 47 north, make a right turn
- ☐ Route 47 north has one-way traffic
- ☐ the start of Route 47 north
- ☐ Route 47 has come to an end

Question 68 - Road Signs

What exactly does this sign mean?

☐   There will be an RC flying zone ahead

☐   You're getting close to an airport

☐   In this zone, planes fly at low altitudes

☐   This is the direction in which planes fly

Question 69 - Road Signs

This highway sign indicates

☐   a forthcoming side road

☐   a forthcoming three-way stop

☐   there is a railroad crossing ahead

☐   a side road with restricted access

Question 70 - Road Signs

This symbol indicates

- ☐ a transition
- ☐ a sharp turn
- ☐ an emergency halt
- ☐ a diversion

Question 71 - Road Signs

This publicly displayed sign is

- ☐ on hills, there is a speed limit sign
- ☐ at roundabouts, there is a speed limit sign
- ☐ a sign indicating an interstate route
- ☐ a speed limit sign on expressways

Question 72 - Road Signs

Which of the following signs denotes a school zone?

A B C D

☐   D

☐   C

☐   B

☐   A

Question 73 - Road Signs

What does this stop sign mean?

☐   In 1,000 feet, there will be construction

☐   After 1,000 feet, turning right is prohibited

☐   An alternate route is available 1,000 feet ahead

☐   There will be a parking zone ahead

Question 74 - Road Signs

This symbol indicates

☐   a median is on the way.

☐   there is a bump in the road ahead

☐   a steep incline awaits

☐   the road ahead has an incline

Question 75 - Road Signs

What does this signal indicate?

☐   You must not take a right turn

☐   You must not walk

☐   Do not combine

☐   Do not proceed

Question 76 - Road Signs

These pavement markings denote

☐ except when turning left, vehicles must not cross the solid yellow line

☐ except to pass, vehicles must not cross the solid yellow line

☐ under no circumstances should a vehicle cross the broken white lines

☐ none of the aforementioned

Question 77 - Road Signs

What exactly does this sign mean?

☐ Stop ahead

☐ A pedestrian zone ahead

☐ Turn right ahead

☐ Flag person ahead

Question 78 - Road Signs

This symbol indicates

- ☐ traffic is merging ahead
- ☐ the terminus of a divided highway
- ☐ a two-way street
- ☐ a narrow street

Question 79 - Road Signs

What exactly does this sign mean?

- ☐ A narrow bridge lies ahead
- ☐ There's an acceleration lane ahead
- ☐ Hidden traffic is ahead
- ☐ The road ahead is narrow

Question 80 - Road Signs

What does this sign mean?

☐   The left lane comes to an end ahead

☐   The right lane comes to an end ahead

☐   A one-way street awaits

☐   A narrow bridge awaits you ahead

Question 81 - Road Signs

A flashing red light indicates that you must_____ before proceeding.

☐   slow down

☐   turn and drive carefully

☐   stop

☐   not stop

Question 82 - Road Signs

This figure's single broken (dashed) white line denotes

- ☐ traffic flowing in opposing directions

- ☐ all traffic is moving in the same direction

- ☐ the road's shoulder

- ☐ a section of a road where passing is prohibited

Question 83 - Road Signs

What does this sign mean?

- ☐ A school area

- ☐ A flagger in a construction zone

- ☐ A road crew at work

- ☐ At an intersection, there is a pedestrian crosswalk

Question 84 - Road Signs

What is the significance of this warning sign?

☐ There will be a stop sign ahead

☐ A yield sign is on the way

☐ Slow-moving vehicles should not follow the directions

☐ Slow-moving vehicles should follow directions

Question 85 - Road Signs

This sign warns drivers about

☐ a bus stop for students

☐ a play area for children

☐ a school zone

☐ the pedestrian crosswalks at an intersection

Question 86 - Road Signs

What is the significance of this regulatory sign?

◻   Do not merge to the left

◻   You must take a right

◻   Right turns are not permitted

◻   Turning left is not permitted

Question 87 - Road Signs

The number depicted in this sign stands for

◻   a sign indicating a U.S. route

◻   an exit number

◻   the distance from the exit

◻   the exit ramp's speed limit

Question 88 - Road Signs

This sign alerts drivers that they

☐   must not leave the pavement

☐   should extend their following distance to 6 seconds

☐   should move quickly onto the shoulder

☐   must move onto the shoulder at a slower pace

Question 89 - Road Signs

What exactly does this sign mean?

☐   Keep to the left of the divider

☐   You're getting close to a divided highway

☐   You'll have to take a detour

☐   Keep to the right of the divider

Question 90 - Road Signs

What exactly does this sign mean?

   ☐   You are not permitted to drive on the railroad tracks

   ☐   A railroad crossing is ahead

   ☐   You have permission to drive on the railroad tracks

   ☐   You must come to a halt at the railroad tracks

Question 91 - Road Signs

What exactly does this sign mean?

   ☐   Pedestrians ahead, no vehicle access

   ☐   Slow down and exercise extreme caution

   ☐   Stop to allow for pedestrians

   ☐   Pedestrians are not permitted to cross

Question 92 - Road Signs

Which of the following signs indicates two-way traffic?

A B C D

- ☐ C
- ☐ D
- ☐ B
- ☐ A

Question 93 - Road Signs

You may travel in the lane indicated by this sign.

- ☐ Only if you're on a bicycle
- ☐ If you're passing the car in front of you
- ☐ If you're on a motorcycle
- ☐ If you're transporting two or more people

Question 94 - Road Signs

What exactly does this sign mean?

☐   There is a Y-intersection ahead

☐   There's a side road ahead

☐   A youth hostel awaits

☐   There is a yield sign ahead

Question 95 - Road Signs

This symbol denotes

☐   the speed limit on the interstate highway

☐   the distance between the current exit and the next

☐   the exit code

☐   the interstate highway number

Question 96 - Road Signs

This sign indicates that the parking spaces are for

☐   elderly people

☐   riders

☐   people with disabilities

☐   patients

Question 97 - Road Signs

What exactly does this road sign mean?

☐   Farmhouse on the way

☐   A cattle crossing is ahead

☐   Following is a veterinary hospital

☐   Next stop, the zoo

Question 98 - Road Signs

What exactly does this sign mean?

◻   It is not permitted to stop or stand

◻   A tunnel is ahead of you

◻   Hitchhiking is not permitted

◻   You're getting close to a school zone

Question 99 - Road Signs

This symbol denotes

◻   the maximum number of vehicles permitted to park

◻   the top speed limit on a road

◻   a checkpoint

◻   a sign indicating a U.S. route marker

92

Question 100 - Road Signs

What does this figure represent?

- ☐ A flag person is ahead, proceed with caution
- ☐ A crew is on the job, so vehicles must slow down
- ☐ There is a pedestrian crossing ahead, vehicles must yield
- ☐ A school crossing is ahead, vehicles must come to a complete stop

Question 101 - Road Signs

What does this sign mean?

- ☐ A high-occupancy vehicle no-passing zone
- ☐ All vehicles are prohibited from passing through this area
- ☐ Trucks are not permitted to pass through this area
- ☐ A school bus no-passing zone

Question 102 - Road Signs

What does this sign mean?

- ☐   Bicyclists are not permitted to be passed by vehicles
- ☐   This road is only for bicyclists to use
- ☐   Bicyclists are not permitted to use this road
- ☐   Bicyclists are not permitted to pass through this area

Question 103 - Road Signs

This symbol is

- ☐   a warning sign in a construction zone
- ☐   a barricade in a construction zone
- ☐   an interstate highway guide sign
- ☐   an object marker on a roadway

Question 104 - Road Signs

It is now 9:30 a.m. Is it legal for you to park next to this sign?

○ Yes, but only for a period of five minutes

○ No

○ Yes, but only if you have a special permit

○ Yes

Question 105 - Road Signs

What does this symbol mean?

○ The road shoulder is significantly lower than the road surface

○ The road is slick and flooded

○ This is a back road

○ The road is strewn with gravel

Question 106 - Road Signs

This sign could be displayed

- [ ] close to hospitals
- [ ] in no-parking zones
- [ ] at intersections
- [ ] in construction zones

Question 107 - Road Signs

What exactly does this sign mean?

- [ ] The railroad ahead of you is closed for maintenance
- [ ] There will be a railroad crossing ahead
- [ ] A new railroad is being built
- [ ] The road ahead is closed for maintenance

Question 108 - Road Signs

When you come across this sign, you're driving at 65 mph. What does it imply?

- ☐ You'll need to slow down ahead
- ☐ You can keep going at your current rate
- ☐ You'll have to pick up the pace
- ☐ You're getting close to a school zone

Question 109 - Road Signs

If you see this sign, you must drive at a speed of at least

- ☐ At least 40 miles per hour
- ☐ At least 50 miles per hour
- ☐ No faster than 50 mph
- ☐ No faster than 40 mph

Question 110 - Road Signs

This steady red X signal above a highway lane indicates that

☐   you are not permitted to drive in this lane

☐   you must only drive in this lane

☐   you are welcome to use this lane

☐   you must come to a complete stop in this lane

Question 111 - Road Signs

What exactly does this sign mean?

☐   Trucks are not permitted to enter or cross this road

☐   Hazardous materials-carrying vehicles may enter or cross this roadway

☐   This roadway may be entered or crossed by high-occupancy vehicles

☐   Trucks may enter or exit this road

Question 112 - Road Signs

What exactly does this sign mean?

- ☐ Drivers may need to shift into a lower gear due to the steep descent ahead
- ☐ A narrow road near a hill, drivers must proceed cautiously
- ☐ There will be a bump ahead, drivers must maintain a consistent speed
- ☐ A freeway acceleration ramp, drivers must merge with freeway traffic

Question 113 - Road Signs

This symbol indicates that

- ☐ there will be an intersection with US Route 22 ahead
- ☐ the following exit is 22 miles away
- ☐ Exit 22 is just ahead
- ☐ Mileage 22 is up ahead

Question 114 - Road Signs

What does this sign mean?

☐   A winding road lies ahead

☐   A narrow bridge awaits you ahead

☐   There is a narrow road ahead

☐   There's a low clearance ahead

Question 115 - Road Signs

What does this sign mean?

☐   There will be two-way traffic ahead

☐   Lane crossing is permitted

☐   A one-way street awaits

☐   There will be an expressway or freeway ahead

Question 116 - Road Signs

This sign indicates that you are permitted to

☐   turn to the left

☐   make a right

☐   make a U-turn

☐   continue straight

Question 117 - Road Signs

What does this sign mean?

☐   You must proceed straight

☐   You must take a right

☐   You have the option of continuing straight or turning right

☐   You have the option of continuing straight or turning left

Question 118 - Road Signs

What exactly does this sign mean?

□   You're headed in the wrong direction

□   The road ahead has been closed

□   A deserted road awaits you ahead

□   You are not permitted to enter

Question 119 - Road Signs

What exactly does this sign mean?

□   The lane is only for right turns

□   The lane is shared by both directions of travel for left turns

□   The lane is for high-speed vehicles only

□   The lane is designated for specific purposes or vehicles

Question 120 - Road Signs

What exactly does this road sign mean?

☐ Continue straight

☐ It denotes the direction

☐ There is a rest area to the right

☐ Prepare to halt

Question 121 - Road Signs

What exactly does this sign mean?

☐ There is a traffic merging area ahead, please come to a complete stop before merging

☐ U-turns are permitted here, please drive slowly

☐ Proceed with caution as there is a one-way road ahead

☐ There will be a roundabout ahead, so be prepared to yield to traffic

Question 122 - Road Signs

What exactly does this sign mean?

- ☐ At an intersection ahead, there is a traffic signal
- ☐ A railroad crossing has a stop sign ahead
- ☐ A stop sign at an intersection is ahead
- ☐ None of the preceding

Question 123 - Road Signs

What exactly does this sign mean?

- ☐ Beyond this sign, farm equipment is not permitted
- ☐ A slick road awaits. use special tires
- ☐ Farm machinery could be on the road
- ☐ Vehicles must slow down as they approach a country road

Question 124 - Road Signs

What does this sign mean?

☐   Right-hand curve

☐   Turn sharply to the right

☐   There is no right turn

☐   Right-hand traffic merges

Question 125 - Road Signs

This posted sign can be found at

☐   intersections

☐   residential zones

☐   exit ramps from freeways

☐   crossings at schools

Question 126 - Road Signs

You have arrived at an intersection with this sign. When are you going to be able to turn right here?

- ☐ When no other vehicles are on the way
- ☐ Never
- ☐ When you see a green light or a green arrow
- ☐ When you come to a complete stop, yield to pedestrians and other vehicles

Question 127 - Road Signs

What does this sign mean?

- ☐ You're getting close to exit 444
- ☐ You're 444 miles from the state line and the end of the road
- ☐ You've arrived at Route 444
- ☐ It denotes none of the preceding

Question 128 - Road Signs

What does this signal indicate?

☐   You've arrived at an abandoned railroad track.

☐   You've arrived at a railroad crossing.

☐   There is a railroad track parallel to the road ahead.

☐   You've arrived at a train station.

Question 129 - Road Signs

This object is used as

☐   a reflector for the night

☐   a radar gun used by a cop

☐   a sign indicating an interstate route

☐   a traffic signal

Question 130 - Road Signs

The broken white lines on the road indicate that

- ☐ there is no passing
- ☐ traffic flows in the opposite direction
- ☐ passing is permissible if done safely
- ☐ bicyclists and motorcyclists use the left lane

Question 131 - Road Signs

This symbol is used for

- ☐ indicating the path to a hospital
- ☐ displaying alternate routes in the event of road closures or construction
- ☐ displaying the designated routes
- ☐ displaying tourist routes

Question 132 - Road Signs

Which of the following pavement markings separates two lanes of traffic traveling in the same direction?

- ☐ B
- ☐ A
- ☐ C
- ☐ None of the preceding

Question 133 - Road Signs

What does this stop sign mean?

- ☐ Do not take a left or a straight path
- ☐ Continue straight
- ☐ Merge to the left
- ☐ Turn left or continue straight

Question 134 - Road Signs

This symbol indicates

☐   the road ahead is permanently closed.

☐   only people with disabilities are permitted to park.

☐   parking is not permitted.

☐   U-turns are not permitted.

Question 135 - Road Signs

What exactly does this sign mean?

☐   You need to change lanes

☐   You must proceed straight

☐   You must halt

☐   You must take a left

Question 136 - Road Signs

What exactly do these yellow pavement markings indicate?

- ☐ This is a three-way intersection
- ☐ Right turns are permitted for vehicles traveling in either direction
- ☐ Left turns are permitted for vehicles traveling in either direction
- ☐ It's a one-way street

Question 137 - Road Signs

This symbol is

- ☐ a stop symbol
- ☐ a yield symbol
- ☐ a sign that says 'Do Not Enter'
- ☐ a sign indicating a work zone

Question 138 - Road Signs

What exactly does this sign mean?

   ☐   This lane allows you to turn left

   ☐   From this lane, you must make a U-turn

   ☐   You must proceed straight and detour at the intersection

   ☐   You have the option of making a U-turn from this lane

Question 139 - Road Signs

What exactly does this sign mean?

   ☐   There will be a traffic merge ahead, stop and then proceed

   ☐   Except for buses, right lane exits

   ☐   The road bends ahead, slow down to a safe speed

   ☐   A narrow bridge lies ahead, proceed with caution

Question 140 - Road Signs

When is it legal to drive in a lane with this sign?

- ☐   If you need to get somewhere quickly

- ☐   Only if you have at least one passenger

- ☐   Only if you have at least two passengers

- ☐   If you are in charge of a truck

Question 141 - Road Signs

This road sign indicates

- ☐   there is a traffic light ahead

- ☐   there is a stop sign ahead

- ☐   there is a roundabout ahead

- ☐   there is a yield sign ahead

Question 142 - Road Signs

This regulatory symbol denotes

☐   a two-way street

☐   a right-turn lane with two lanes

☐   traffic merging in both directions

☐   a two-way left-turn lane

Question 143 - Road Signs

What exactly does this sign mean?

☐   There will be a work zone ahead of you

☐   There will be a hiccup in the road ahead

☐   There will be a low place in the road ahead

☐   There will be a detour ahead

Question 144 - Road Signs

This symbol indicates

☐ Vehicles must maintain a speed of at least 40 miles per hour

☐ Slow-moving vehicles are not permitted to exceed 40 mph

☐ Vehicles are not permitted to exceed the posted speed limit of 40 mph

☐ Vehicles must travel at a speed of fewer than 40 miles per hour

Question 145 - Road Signs

What do these two arrows represent?

☐ Start of a divided highway

☐ End of a divided highway

☐ Two-way traffic ahead

☐ Traffic to flow on both sides.

Question 146 - Road Signs

What exactly does this sign mean?

◻   There is a left turn ahead of you

◻   Turning left is not permitted

◻   A series of curves lie ahead

◻   A side road is entering from the right

Question 147 - Road Signs

What exactly does this sign mean?

◻   The speed limit posted for a sharp right turn

◻   The recommended minimum speed on a highway

◻   A safe speed indication for a right curve ahead.

◻   The speed limit posted for an S-shaped curve

Question 148 - Road Signs

The arrow on this sign indicates that

- ☐ drivers have the option of going in either direction
- ☐ all traffic must proceed only in the direction indicated by the arrow
- ☐ the lane ahead is designated for trucks turning right
- ☐ to make a right turn, all vehicles must come to a complete stop

Question 149 - Road Signs

If you see this sign and are traveling slower than the majority of traffic, you should

- ☐ accelerate your pace
- ☐ enter the left lane
- ☐ put yourself in the right lane
- ☐ take the next available exit

The availability of_____ is represented by this blue sign.

☐   food

☐   lodging

☐   gas station

☐   telephones

SITUATIONS AND SIGNS

Here you will find a collection of Signs and Situations that will help you sharpen your knowledge about intersections and shared lanes.

Total Questions: 50
Correct Answer to pass: 40

Question 1 - Signs and Situations

What exactly does this sign mean?

☐   A divided highway begins ahead of you

☐   There is a hazard ahead, proceed to the left or right

☐   At the next intersection, take a left or a right

☐   A Y-intersection is ahead

Question 2 - Signs and Situations

This symbol indicates

- ☐ there is a bridge ahead, the road width is 13 feet 6 inches
- ☐ there is a parking area ahead, the road width is 13 feet 6 inches
- ☐ there is an underpass ahead with a vertical clearance of 13 feet 6 inches
- ☐ there is a median ahead, the road width is 13 feet 6 inches

Question 3 - Signs and Situations

You've arrived at an intersection with a stop sign. Where must you draw the line?

- ☐ Before the crosswalk
- ☐ Before the stop line
- ☐ Before approaching the intersection
- ☐ Whichever of the aforementioned options you arrive at first

Question 4 - Signs and Situations

At around the same time, two cars arrive at an uncontrolled intersection (one without signs or signals). Which of the following statements is correct?

☐   Car A must yield to its right

☐   Due to Car A turning onto a new road, it has the right-of-way

☐   The drivers should decide who has the right of way

☐   Car B must yield to the right

Question 5 - Signs and Situations

Which of the following statements about headlights is NOT CORRECT?

☐   When using your windshield wipers continuously in bad weather, you must use your headlights

☐   From half an hour after sunset to half an hour before sunrise, you must use your headlights

☐   You may drive with your parking lights on to make your vehicle more visible

☐   When visibility is 500 feet or less, you must use your headlights

Question 6 - Signs and Situations

This road's center lane is separated from the other lanes by solid and broken yellow lines. This lane is intended for

- ☐ turning to the left
- ☐ parking
- ☐ passing
- ☐ emergency stops

Question 7 - Signs and Situations

What exactly does this sign mean?

- ☐ Slow down and proceed with caution because there is a school zone crossing ahead
- ☐ Prepare to stop at the crosswalk ahead
- ☐ Slow down and keep an eye out for pedestrians on the shared section of road ahead
- ☐ Slow down and keep an eye out for pedestrians as you approach a park or playground

Question 8 - Signs and Situations

You're following another car. What is the recommended minimum following distance behind the vehicle in front of you?

- ☐ 40 feet
- ☐ 2 seconds
- ☐ 4 seconds
- ☐ One car length, for every ten miles per hour of speed

Question 9 - Signs and Situations

A car has been parked in front of a fire hydrant. Is this legally allowed?

- ☐ No, you are not permitted to park within 30 feet of a fire hydrant
- ☐ Yes, if it is moved within 10 minutes.
- ☐ Yes
- ☐ No, you are not permitted to park within 15 feet of a fire hydrant

Question 10 - Signs and Situations

This symbol indicates

- ☐ there is a double curve ahead
- ☐ there is a sharp right turn ahead
- ☐ there is a right-hand curve ahead
- ☐ a winding road lies ahead

Question 11 - Signs and Situations

What should you do if you see a steady yellow traffic light?

- ☐ Come to a halt, if it is safe to do so
- ☐ Proceed with caution because a hazard may be ahead
- ☐ Accelerate to clear the signal before it turns red
- ☐ Stop, yield to oncoming traffic and continue when it is safe to do so

Question 12 - Signs and Situations

You've arrived at a crossroads. You want to make a left and have a green light. Can you go ahead?

- ☐ Yes, because this is a 'protected' turn, you will have the right-of-way
- ☐ Yes, but you must first yield to oncoming traffic and pedestrians
- ☐ No, you can only turn left when there is a green arrow
- ☐ Yes, but only if there is a sign indicating that a left turn is permitted

Question 13 - Signs and Situations

This driver is signaling with his hand. The driver plans to

- ☐ accelerate
- ☐ take a right.
- ☐ take a left.
- ☐ stop or slow down.

Question 14 - Signs and Situations

What does this sign mean?

- ☐ Merging from the right
- ☐ The conclusion of a divided highway
- ☐ From the left, merge
- ☐ Two-way street traffic

Question 15 - Signs and Situations

This driver is signaling with his hand. The driver plans to

- ☐ take a right
- ☐ take a left
- ☐ accelerate
- ☐ stop or slow down

Question 16 - Signs and Situations

What does this sign mean?

- ☐ There will be one-way traffic ahead

- ☐ The divided highway comes to an end ahead

- ☐ Traffic is congealing ahead

- ☐ A divided highway begins ahead of you

Question 17 - Signs and Situations

Which of the following railroad crossing statements is CORRECT?

- ☐ You must come to a complete stop at a flashing, red railroad signal until it is safe to proceed

- ☐ You may only drive through a railroad crossing gate if it is fully raised

- ☐ If you must stop at a railroad crossing, you must do so within 15-to-50 feet of the tracks

- ☐ All of the preceding statements are correct

Question 18 - Signs and Situations

When changing lanes, which of the following actions is optional?

- ☐ Examining your mirrors

- ☐ Signaling

- ☐ Checking behind your back

- ☐ None of the preceding

Question 19 - Signs and Situations

At about the same time, two cars arrive at a four-way stop. Which car should be the first to leave?

- ☐   Car B, as Car B is to the right of Car A
- ☐   Car A, because it is on the opposite side of the road from Car B
- ☐   As decided by the drivers
- ☐   Car A should go first, because it is turning onto a new road

Question 20 - Signs and Situations

On an open road, you notice a school bus stopped ahead, its red lights flashing and its stop arm extended. So, what should you do now?

- ☐   No matter which way you're going, come to a complete stop
- ☐   If you are traveling in the same direction as the school bus, you must come to a complete stop
- ☐   Reduce your speed to 10 mph and proceed with caution
- ☐   Stop, give way to pedestrians and then proceed cautiously

Question 21 - Signs and Situations

You're about to reach an intersection where you want to turn left. There are no other vehicles visible. Is it still necessary to signal?

- ☐ Yes, even if only briefly, you must use your turn signals
- ☐ Yes, you must turn on your turn signals at least 100 feet before making a turn
- ☐ No, turn signals are only required when other vehicles are present
- ☐ No, turn signals are not required

Question 22 - Signs and Situations

On a red light, you're about to make a right turn. A pedestrian begins to cross the road into which you intend to enter. So, what should you do now?

- ☐ Pass the pedestrian, merge into the far lane
- ☐ Alert the pedestrian to your presence, sound your horn
- ☐ Increase your speed to pass the pedestrian
- ☐ Allow the pedestrian to cross

Question 23 - Signs and Situations

You're in the right lane of a four-lane highway with a posted speed limit of 50 miles per hour. A police car with its lights flashing comes to a stop ahead of you. So, what should you do now?

- ☐ Proceed with extreme caution
- ☐ Reduce your speed to 35 mph or less and if possible, move into a non-adjacent lane
- ☐ If possible, move into a non-adjacent lane, otherwise, slow down to 35 mph or less
- ☐ Reduce your speed to 25 mph and proceed with caution

Question 24 - Signs and Situations

What does this sign mean?

- ☐ Vehicles in the left lane must make a left turn, while vehicles in the right lane must make a right turn
- ☐ Vehicles in the left lane must turn left, while those in the right lane must continue straight
- ☐ Vehicles in the left lane must merge left, while those in the right lane must merge right
- ☐ Vehicles in the left lane must turn left, while vehicles in the right lane may either continue straight or turn right

Question 25 - Signs and Situations

At about the same time, two cars arrive at an intersection. Which of the following statements is the most accurate?

- ☐ Car A must yield because it is making a left turn
- ☐ Car B is required to yield to turning vehicles
- ☐ Due to Car A turning, it must yield
- ☐ The drivers must decide which of them will go first

Question 26 - Signs and Situations

Three cars arrive at an intersection just as a pedestrian cross one of the roads. Who has the right of way in this situation?

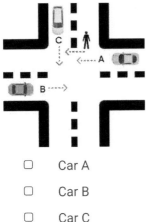

☐   Car A

☐   Car B

☐   Car C

☐   Pedestrian

Question 27 - Signs and Situations

You come to an intersection and see this sign. So, what should you do now?

☐   Stop completely, give way to pedestrians and traffic ahead and then proceed

☐   Maintain your speed because all traffic in front of you must yield to you

☐   Slow down and prepare to yield to oncoming traffic, but you will not be required to stop

☐   Slow down and prepare to yield to oncoming pedestrians and traffic

Question 28 - Signs and Situations

Which vehicles are hidden in the truck's blind spots (also known as 'No-Zones')?

☐ Vehicle A

☐ Vehicle C

☐ Vehicles A and B

☐ Vehicle B

Question 29 - Signs and Situations

Two cars arrived at an intersection around the same time. Which of the following statements is correct?

☐ Car A must yield because it is making a left turn.

☐ The first car has the right-of-way, the second car must then yield

☐ The other driver must be waved through by one of the drivers

☐ Due to Car B turning right, it must yield

Question 30 - Signs and Situations

A car is parked 15 feet from a railroad. Is this car parked legally?

☐ No, you are not permitted to park within 100 feet of a railroad crossing

☐ Yes, as long as you stay behind the stop line, you can park near a railroad crossing

☐ No, you are not permitted to park within 50 feet of a railroad crossing

☐ Yes, as long as you're not on the tracks, you can park near a railroad crossing

Question 31 - Signs and Situations

Which of the following statements about hydroplaning is correct?

☐ A gust of wind can cause a hydroplaning car to spin out of control

☐ At speeds as low as 35 mph, your tires can begin to hydroplane

☐ If your vehicle begins to hydroplane, you should slow down

☐ All of the preceding statements are correct

Question 32 - Signs and Situations

This driver is signaling with his hand. The driver intends to

☐ turn right

☐ stop or slow down

☐ accelerate

☐ take a left

Question 33 - Signs and Situations

Which of the following statements regarding railroad crossings is correct?

☐ A gate can be driven through before it is fully raised

☐ If you must stop, make sure you are at least 15 feet away from the tracks

☐ You can cross the tracks as soon as the train has passed if there is no fence

☐ All of the preceding statements are correct

Question 34 - Signs and Situations

What exactly does this sign mean?

- ☐ The top speed is 50 miles per hour
- ☐ The minimum speed limit is 50 miles per hour
- ☐ At night, the speed limit is 50 mph
- ☐ The recommended speed limit is 50 miles per hour

Question 35 - Signs and Situations

What exactly does this sign mean?

- ☐ A two-way, left-turn lane begins ahead of you
- ☐ The divided highway comes to an end ahead
- ☐ A divided highway begins ahead of you
- ☐ Ahead, left turns are not permitted

Question 36 - Signs and Situations

When is it legal to turn left at a red light?

- ☐ Never
- ☐ Only when turning from a one-way street onto another one-way street
- ☐ Only when turning from a one-way street onto a different street
- ☐ Unless otherwise stated, at any time

Question 37 - Signs and Situations

Is it legal to turn right at a red light?

- ☐ Yes, but only after coming to a complete stop and yielding to pedestrians and traffic
- ☐ Yes, because this is a 'protected' turn, you will have the right-of-way
- ☐ No, you cannot turn right at a red light
- ☐ Yes, but only if a sign permits you to

Question 38 - Signs and Situations

You parked on a steep incline with no curb. Which way should your front wheels be pointed?

- ☐ Towards the road's edge
- ☐ Straight
- ☐ Away from the road's edge
- ☐ Any direction is possible

Question 39 - Signs and Situations

Two vehicles are making a left turn onto a divided highway. Which vehicles are turning properly?

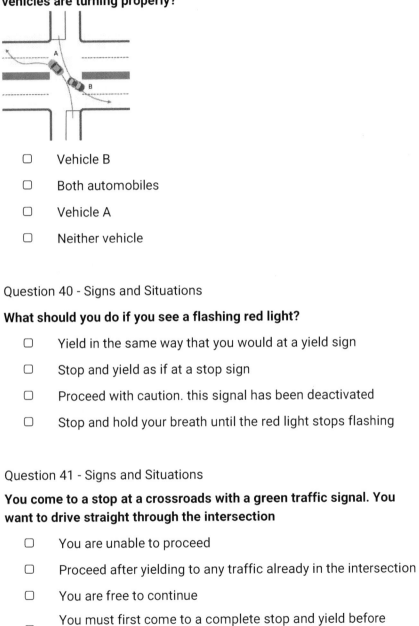

- ☐ Vehicle B
- ☐ Both automobiles
- ☐ Vehicle A
- ☐ Neither vehicle

Question 40 - Signs and Situations

What should you do if you see a flashing red light?

- ☐ Yield in the same way that you would at a yield sign
- ☐ Stop and yield as if at a stop sign
- ☐ Proceed with caution. this signal has been deactivated
- ☐ Stop and hold your breath until the red light stops flashing

Question 41 - Signs and Situations

You come to a stop at a crossroads with a green traffic signal. You want to drive straight through the intersection

- ☐ You are unable to proceed
- ☐ Proceed after yielding to any traffic already in the intersection
- ☐ You are free to continue
- ☐ You must first come to a complete stop and yield before proceeding

Question 42 - Signs and Situations

What exactly does this sign mean?

☐   Trucks transporting dangerous materials may enter the road

☐   Heavy vehicles may enter the road

☐   Fire trucks may have to enter the road

☐   Farm vehicles might enter the roadway

Question 43 - Signs and Situations

Car B has entered an intersection to make a right turn on a red light. Car A has a green light and wishes to proceed through the intersection. Which of the following statements is correct?

☐   Car A should accelerate to pass Car B

☐   Car A must give way to Car B

☐   Car B must come to a halt and allow Car A to pass

☐   None of the preceding statements is correct.

Question 44 - Signs and Situations

You notice an emergency vehicle approaching with flashing lights. So, what should you do now?

☐   Take it easy

☐   Accelerate and look for a safe place to turn off

☐   Pull over to the side of the road and come to a complete stop

☐   Keep your speed and direction constant

Question 45 - Signs and Situations

What exactly does this sign mean?

☐   At night, the speed limit is 35 mph

☐   During the day, the speed limit is 35 mph

☐   The top speed is 35 miles per hour

☐   The recommended speed limit is 35 miles per hour

Question 46 - Signs and Situations

Whom should you yield before turning left into a driveway?

- ☐ Pedestrians and oncoming traffic
- ☐ Oncoming traffic, but not pedestrians
- ☐ Oncoming vehicles, but not pedestrians
- ☐ Neither pedestrians nor oncoming vehicles.

Question 47 - Signs and Situations

You've parked next to a curb and are facing uphill. Which way should your front wheels be pointed?

- ☐ Any possible direction
- ☐ Away from the curb
- ☐ Towards the curb
- ☐ Straight

Question 48 - Signs and Situations

When must you dim your high-beam headlights?

- ☐ When you're within 1,000 feet of another vehicle
- ☐ Whenever you are within 500 feet of an oncoming vehicle or within 200 feet of another vehicle which you are following
- ☐ Whenever you are within 200 feet of an oncoming vehicle or within 500 feet of another vehicle which you are following
- ☐ When you're within 500 feet of another vehicle

Question 49 - Signs and Situations

You come to an intersection and see this sign. So, what should you do now?

☐ Before proceeding, come to a complete stop and yield to traffic

☐ Come to a complete stop before proceeding

☐ You can't go through here, find another way

☐ Reduce your speed and proceed only if the intersection is clear

Question 50 - Signs and Situations

Which of the following commands has precedence (i.e., should be followed above all others)?

☐ A cautionary sign

☐ A STOP indication

☐ A traffic light

☐ A police officer

FINES & LIMITS

This section is specific to your State and you will find 10 questions on Fines and Limits here. It is one of the most difficult sections and the one that most people fail.

Total Questions: 10
Correct Answer to pass: 8

Question 1 - Fines & Limits

A learner's license holder under the age of 18 must complete at least _____ hours of driving experience before being given a driver license.

- ☐ 25
- ☐ 10
- ☐ 50
- ☐ 30

Question 2 - Fines & Limits

Which of the following is the non-commercial driver's license class?

- ☐ A
- ☐ B
- ☐ E
- ☐ C

Question 3 - Fines & Limits

While you have a learner's license, you must drive under the supervision of a person who_____

☐   has reached the age of 21

☐   possesses a valid driver's license

☐   sits beside you

☐   satisfies all of the preceding conditions

Question 4 - Fines & Limits

Your license will be canceled if you are found guilty of at least _____offences that add points to your driving record within five years.

☐   10

☐   15

☐   20

☐   5

Question 5 - Fines & Limits

A Class E driver license can only be obtained if you are at least _____years old.

☐   21

☐   15

☐   16

☐   18

Question 6 - Fines & Limits

When do you need to get Bodily Injury Liability (BIL) insurance for your car?

☐ If you were the cause of an accident that resulted in injuries

☐ If you were convicted of DUI

☐ Your license was suspended due to too many points

☐ If any of the aforementioned events occurred

Question 7 - Fines & Limits

Your license will be suspended for up to a year if you acquire _____points in a 36-month period.

☐ 48

☐ 24

☐ 60

☐ 36

Question 8 - Fines & Limits

If you are required to obtain Bodily Injury Liability (BIL) insurance coverage for your car but fail to do so, you may be subject to which of the following penalties?

☐ (a) Your driver's license may be suspended

☐ (a) Your vehicle may be seized

☐ (c) The license plates on your vehicle may be suspended

☐ (a) in addition (c)

Question 9 - Fines & Limits

If you are convicted of DUI for the third time, you will have your license revoked for at least

       ☐   five years

       ☐   200 days

       ☐   one year

       ☐   180-day period

Question 10 - Fines & Limits

If a driver under the age of 18 is found guilty of driving unattended during restricted hours, he or she will accumulate_____ points on his or her driving record.

       ☐   4

       ☐   5

       ☐   6

       ☐   3

DISTRACTED DRIVING TEST

This is one of the most crucial sections. You'll be asked about modern driving distractions, as well as, driving while under the influence of drugs and pharmaceuticals.

Total Questions: 25
Correct Answer to pass: 20

Question 1 - Distracted Driving

You should be cautious of the various distractions and limitations listed below -

- ☐ Listening to extremely loud music or using technologies like cell phones, GPS and intercoms
- ☐ Changing your vehicle's electronic controls
- ☐ Alcohol, drugs and some medications
- ☐ Everything mentioned above

Question 2 - Distracted Driving

What other medications, besides alcohol, can impair a person's ability to drive safely?

- ☐ Medications available over-the-counter
- ☐ Prescribed medication
- ☐ Medications used to treat headaches, colds, hay fever or other allergies, as well as, those used to relax the nerves
- ☐ Everything mentioned above

Question 3 - Distracted Driving

You're behind the wheel and a problem in the rear seat requires your attention. You must:

- ☐ Turn around and cope with the situation, occasionally looking ahead
- ☐ Before dealing with the matter, pull over to the side of the road and park your vehicle
- ☐ Adjust the rearview mirror to see what's in the back seat
- ☐ Slow down and deal with the matter while you're driving

Question 4 - Distracted Driving

Which of the following will NOT keep you from being distracted while driving?

- ☐ You could save your favorite radio stations by pre-programming them
- ☐ Pre-loosening the lid of your coffee cup
- ☐ Pre-planning your trip
- ☐ Before you begin, make sure that all of your mirrors are adjusted

Question 5 - Distracted Driving

What should you do if you feel drowsy before driving?

- ☐ Listen to music
- ☐ Coffee Drinking
- ☐ Exercise
- ☐ Sleeping

Question 6 - Distracted Driving

Drivers must _____ to keep awake when driving to overcome highway hypnosis, drowsiness and tiredness.

☐ Take stimulants

☐ Use the cell phone

☐ Message someone

☐ Exercise the eyes

Question 7 - Distracted Driving

Which of the following is NOT an adequate way to drive?

☐ Using visual, display gadgets and texting while driving

☐ When driving, use side mirrors

☐ Listening to music while driving

☐ While parking, look both front and sideways

Question 8 - Distracted Driving

Is it legal for teenage drivers to talk on their cell phones while driving?

☐ Only when traveling at less than 25 mph

☐ Yes, as long as you're cautious

☐ It is illegal to talk on a cell phone while driving

☐ Only if you're on a country road

Question 9 - Distracted Driving

You don't want to be a distracted driver, therefore

☐ when there are no other vehicles around you, browse maps or use your phone

☐ turn off your phone till you get to your location

☐ have all of your highly emotional conversations during the first hour of driving

☐ smoke, eat and drink, on straight sections of the road

Question 10 - Distracted Driving

Which of the statements below is correct?

☐ It is safe and time-saving to have lunch while driving

☐ While driving, you can send and read brief texts

☐ If you get lost while driving, you can rapidly write navigation instructions

☐ Using audio navigation while driving is legal

Question 11 - Distracted Driving

Can you take drugs before getting behind the wheel?

☐ Only with a prescription

☐ No

☐ Only over-the-counter medications

☐ Only if the doctor believes it won't impair your ability to drive safely

Question 12 - Distracted Driving

Talking on a cell phone while driving increases your chances of getting involved in a crash by:

- ☐ Up to twice as much
- ☐ An additional sum
- ☐ Up to three times as much
- ☐ As much as four times

Question 13 - Distracted Driving

Is it safe to drive while holding something in your lap?

- ☐ Never, ever
- ☐ Yes, as long as it's not a human or a pet
- ☐ Yes, if it's a small animal
- ☐ Yes, as long as you don't get distracted

Question 14 - Distracted Driving

Things that can keep you from paying attention to the road include:

- ☐ Texting and talking on the phone
- ☐ Checking blind spots
- ☐ Checking the traffic behind you regularly
- ☐ Always looking in the mirror

Question 15 - Distracted Driving

Is it illegal to text while driving?

- ☐ Yes, it is illegal
- ☐ It's legal as long as you don't go faster than 15 mph
- ☐ No, it is legal
- ☐ Only when you come to a complete stop at a stop sign, is it legal

Question 16 - Distracted Driving

Which medicines can impair your ability to drive safely?

- ☐ Medications available over-the-counter
- ☐ Illegal drugs
- ☐ Prescription medications
- ☐ Everything mentioned above

Question 17 - Distracted Driving

Which of the following statements about cell phones is correct?

- ☐ If you get a call while driving, slow down and take the call
- ☐ Adult drivers are permitted to use a hands-free cell phone while driving
- ☐ Adult drivers are permitted to use a hand-held cell phone while driving
- ☐ Calling while driving saves time

Question 18 - Distracted Driving

A juvenile driver receives a phone call on his or her cell phone. He or she must:

- ☐ Not carry a cell phone when driving.
- ☐ Answer the phone in an emergency
- ☐ Not pick up the phone
- ☐ Answer the phone, utilizing a hands-free cell phone.

Question 19 – Distracted Driving

How can sleep deprivation affect your driving?

- ☐ Impaired decision-making
- ☐ Slower response times
- ☐ Reduced awareness
- ☐ Everything mentioned above

Question 20 - Distracted Driving

Which of these will not negatively impact your driving while you're on the road?

- ☐ Listening to the radio
- ☐ Drinking coffee
- ☐ Smoking
- ☐ Eating a sandwich

DRINKING AND DRIVING TEST

This section discusses the consequences of drinking and driving. Be sure to understand the limitations and the effects of alcohol on your body.

Total Questions: 25
Correct Answer to pass: 20

Question 1 - Drinking and Driving

Which of the following is prohibited for minors?

☐   Having a blood alcohol concentration (BAC) of 0.02 percent or higher

☐   Attempting to buy alcohol

☐   Drinking alcohol

☐   Everything mentioned above

Question 2 - Drinking and Driving

Which of the following has the most alcohol?

☐   A 5-oz glass of 12% wine

☐   A 1.5-oz shot of 80 proof liquor

☐   A 12-oz glass of 5% beer

☐   They're all the same

Question 3 - Drinking and Driving

Which of the following areas does not allow open containers of alcohol?

- ☐ Passenger areas of standard passenger cars
- ☐ Passenger areas of limousines
- ☐ In the trunk of a passenger car
- ☐ Residential areas of motorhomes

Question 4 - Drinking and Driving

Alcohol might have an impact on your

- ☐ concentration
- ☐ reaction time
- ☐ decision-making process
- ☐ all of the answers above are correct

Question 5 - Drinking and Driving

_____ is the biggest cause of death among Americans aged 16 to 24.

- ☐ Driving while under the influence of alcohol
- ☐ Cancer
- ☐ Obesity
- ☐ Overdose from drugs

Question 6 - Drinking and Driving

Factors that impact your blood alcohol concentration (BAC) are

- ☐ The number of alcoholic beverages you've consumed
- ☐ How quickly you drink
- ☐ How much you weigh
- ☐ Everything mentioned above

Question 7 - Drinking and Driving

Which of the following beverages has a 1.5-ounce amount of alcohol?

- ☐ 1 liter of beer
- ☐ One shot of 80 proof liquor
- ☐ A 5-oz. glass of wine
- ☐ Each of the above

Question 8 - Drinking and Driving

It is especially risky to drink alcohol and drive at night because:

- ☐ At night, the roadways are crowded
- ☐ Your field of vision is already limited
- ☐ At night, drinking has a greater impact on your judgment
- ☐ You are more likely to encounter drunk drivers

Question 9 - Drinking and Driving

A drunk motorist is more likely to:

- ☐ Drive too quickly or too slowly
- ☐ Frequently change lanes
- ☐ Fail to dim high lights for oncoming traffic
- ☐ Do all of the above.

Question 10 - Drinking and Driving

Which of the following occurs when a driver's blood alcohol concentration (BAC) rises?

- ☐ Alcohol impairs coordination and muscle control
- ☐ The first processes to be impacted are self-control and judgment
- ☐ Alcohol has a growing impact on the brain of the drinker
- ☐ All of the aforementioned

Question 11 - Drinking and Driving

Which of the following will assist a person under the influence of alcohol in recovering from the effects?

- ☐ Time
- ☐ Cold, fresh air
- ☐ A mug of coffee
- ☐ Everything mentioned above

Question 12 - Drinking and Driving

The concept of implied consent states that by operating a motor vehicle, you have accepted that

- ☐ if a police officer requests it, you will submit to a chemical test
- ☐ you will never drink alcohol or have an open bottle or other container containing alcohol while driving
- ☐ you will always follow the fundamental rules
- ☐ none of the above applies to you

Question 13 - Drinking and Driving

It is unlawful to have open containers of alcohol in a car in which of the following places?

☐   Beneath the seat

☐   The first-row seating

☐   The console

☐   All of the preceding

Question 14 - Drinking and Driving

Which of the following is NOT an alcohol effect?

☐   Erroneous judgment

☐   Vision impairment

☐   Slower reaction times

☐   Increased vigilance

Question 15 - Drinking and Driving

Driving and drinking

☐   diminishes your reflexes

☐   reduces a driver's awareness of potential hazards on the road

☐   reduces physical control of a vehicle

☐   does everything mentioned above

Question 16 - Drinking and Driving

Which of the following is an acceptable substitute for drinking and driving?

- ☐   Public transports
- ☐   A designated driver
- ☐   A taxicab
- ☐   Any of the preceding

Question 17 - Drinking and Driving

If you are convicted of driving under the influence of alcohol or drugs, you may face the penalties listed below.

- ☐   Community service
- ☐   Suspension of your driver's license
- ☐   Severe fines and increased insurance rates
- ☐   Any or all of the preceding

Question 18 - Drinking and Driving

Which of the following statements about drivers under the age of twenty-one is correct?

- ☐   They are permitted to consume small amounts of alcohol, but not while driving
- ☐   They can purchase alcohol but are not permitted to consume it
- ☐   They are permitted to have trace levels of alcohol in their blood while driving
- ☐   They are not permitted to purchase, consume or be in possession of alcohol

Question 19 - Drinking and Driving

How many standard servings of alcohol can an adult safely drink before driving?

- ☐ 2
- ☐ It depends on the person
- ☐ 1
- ☐ 3

Question 20 - Drinking and Driving

Which of the following is an effect of drinking on your ability to drive?

- ☐ Reduces driving ability
- ☐ It slows reflexes
- ☐ It negatively impacts one's depth perception
- ☐ Everything mentioned above

Question 21 - Drinking and Driving

Which of the following has no effect on blood alcohol content?

- ☐ Body mass index
- ☐ The type of alcohol
- ☐ Timespan during which alcohol was consumed
- ☐ Length of time since the last drink

Question 22 - Drinking and Driving

Which of the below will result in a required suspension of a minor's license?

- ☐ Transporting an open beer container
- ☐ Driving while under the influence of drugs
- ☐ Transporting an open container of alcohol
- ☐ Any or all of the preceding

Question 23 - Drinking and Driving

After drinking a significant amount of alcohol, you can ensure that you will not be driving under the influence if you

- ☐ drank beer or wine but no strong liquor
- ☐ wait at least an hour
- ☐ wait a day or two
- ☐ wait at least 30 minutes

Question 24 - Drinking and Driving

If you are unable to drive your vehicle because of excessive alcohol consumption, you must

- ☐ allow a designated driver to operate your vehicle
- ☐ keep yourself awake when driving by drinking coffee
- ☐ call 911 for assistance with driving
- ☐ before driving, utilize medications to counteract the effects of alcohol

Question 25 - Drinking and Driving

Your driving privileges may be suspended

- ☐   if you refuse to take a blood or urine test

- ☐   if you transport alcoholic beverages in closed containers while working for someone, who has an off-site liquor sales license

- ☐   if you have a full, sealed, unopened container of liquor, beer or wine in your vehicle

- ☐   if you do not appoint a sober driver

EXAM TEST PRACTICE

Welcome to the final part of this book, sit down, relax and get focused. This practice test contains the same number of questions you will find in your official DMV exam.

Total Questions: 50
Correct Answer to pass: 40

Question 1 - Mock Exam

Work zone signs are commonly of this color

☐ orange

☐ blue

☐ green

☐ red

Question 2 - Mock Exam

This symbol is

☐ a traffic light

☐ a sign indicating a work zone

☐ a yield symbol

☐ a sign that says "Do Not Enter"

Question 3 - Mock Exam

Allowing automobiles to slow down and exit expressways is made possible by

- ☐ lanes for acceleration
- ☐ turnpikes
- ☐ roundabouts
- ☐ exit ramps

Question 4 - Mock Exam

If an emergency vehicle with a siren or flashing lights approaches you while driving in a roundabout in Florida, you must

- ☐ stop at the roundabout
- ☐ take the first exit to the right in the roundabout
- ☐ take the first exit to the left in the roundabout
- ☐ proceed to the next exit and pull over

Question 5 - Mock Exam

When passing another car, move as rapidly as possible past the other driver's blind spot

- ☐ by changing gears
- ☐ by simply lowering your speed
- ☐ by raising your speed
- ☐ by not exceeding the speed limit

Question 6 - Mock Exam

If you miss your exit on a limited-access highway, you should take the following precautions:

- ☐   Stop and ask for assistance
- ☐   Return to the exit by backing up
- ☐   Return to the exit by doing a U-turn
- ☐   Proceed to the next exit

Question 7 - Mock Exam

On one-way roads, solid yellow lines are used as

- ☐   lines on the left
- ☐   lines on the right
- ☐   lines in the middle
- ☐   stop lines

Question 8 - Mock Exam

Which of the following right-of-way claims is incorrect?

- ☐   The vehicle on the through route must surrender to vehicles on the terminating road at an open (uncontrolled) T-intersection.
- ☐   All approaching cars must yield to vehicles entering or crossing a roadway from a private driveway.
- ☐   Left-turning vehicles must yield to approaching traffic.
- ☐   In unmarked crosswalks, vehicles must yield to pedestrians.

Question 9 - Mock Exam

You must never pass

☐ if there is an impending slope or a curve with no clear vision

☐ if your lane is bordered by a solid yellow line

☐ A school bus with flashing red lights ahead came to a halt.

☐ in any of the preceding circumstances

Question 10 - Mock Exam

In which direction should you turn the front wheels if your vehicle is skidding?

☐ Towards the right

☐ Towards the left

☐ In the opposite direction of the skid

☐ In the skidding direction

Question 11 - Mock Exam

When descending a steep hill, you should

☐ continue to press the brakes

☐ change to a lower gear

☐ change to a higher gear

☐ activate your emergency flashers

What exactly does this sign mean?

- ☐ Right turns are not permitted
- ☐ Turning left is not permitted
- ☐ Ahead, the left lane is closed
- ☐ Ahead, the right lane is closed

Question 13 - Mock Exam

Turning left from a two-way street onto a one-way street requires you to

- ☐ swing wide to the right before turning
- ☐ begin the turn with your left wheel as near to the yellow dividing line as feasible
- ☐ begin the turn with your right wheel as near to the yellow dividing line as feasible
- ☐ carry out any of the preceding actions

Question 14 - Mock Exam

When it rains heavily, your tires may ride on a layer of water and lose contact with the road. This danger is referred to as

- ☐ hydroplaning
- ☐ rainplaning.
- ☐ waterplaning.
- ☐ friction planning

Question 15 - Mock Exam

It is required to use _____ when the sun is shining brightly or when a line of vehicles following you could obscure your turn signal light.

- ☐   parking lights
- ☐   emergency flashers
- ☐   signal with hand
- ☐   brake lights

Question 16 - Mock Exam

You should use_____ if you are traveling faster than the rest of the traffic on an expressway.

- ☐   a lane in the middle or on the left
- ☐   the correct lane
- ☐   on the shoulder
- ☐   whatever lane

Question 17 - Mock Exam

If you see a pedestrian crossing the street with a white cane (perhaps with a red tip) or a guiding dog, you must

- ☐   come to a complete halt
- ☐   increase your pace and rapidly pass the pedestrian.
- ☐   beep your horn to alert the pedestrian of your presence.
- ☐   slow down and lessen your speed

Question 18 - Mock Exam

If you are being followed too closely or tailgated, what should you do?

- ☐ Slow down and allow the driver in front of you to pass
- ☐ To evade the driver, increase your speed
- ☐ To warn the driver, sound your horn
- ☐ Stop your car on the highway and fight with the motorist

Question 19 - Mock Exam

You may make a _____ if the road is too narrow to make a U-Turn

- ☐ a two-point turn
- ☐ a four-point turn
- ☐ a three-point turn
- ☐ a five-point turn

Question 20 - Mock Exam

If you see a flashing yellow light, you should

- ☐ slow down and proceed with caution
- ☐ continue at the same rate
- ☐ accelerate
- ☐ come to a complete halt

Question 21 - Mock Exam

When backing up your vehicle, what should you do?

☐ Do not rely on your mirrors. Instead, turn your head to peer out the back window

☐ Do not rely on your mirrors. Instead, beep your horn to warn oncoming pedestrians

☐ Rely on your side mirrors

☐ Rely on your rearview mirror

Question 22 - Mock Exam

In a typical work zone sign

☐ letters are black on an orange background

☐ letters are white on a yellow background

☐ letters are white on an orange background

☐ letters are black on a yellow background

Question 23 - Mock Exam

What exactly does this sign mean?

☐ There will be a roundabout ahead

☐ A left turn is required ahead

☐ There will be a parking lot ahead

☐ There will be a highway interchange ahead

When passing a bicycle heading in your direction in Florida, you must leave at least_____ of clearance between your vehicle and the bicycle.

☐   3 feet

☐   10 feet

☐   7 feet

☐   5 feet

Disabled people with placards may park in a _____parking space.

☐   white

☐   red

☐   green

☐   blue

At night, high-beam headlights should be used

☐   on unknown roads especially in construction zones

☐   where there could be people alongside the roadway

☐   whenever no oncoming cars present

☐   Under all of the above circumstances

Question 27 - Mock Exam

The freeway section beyond the solid white line is designated for

☐   only U-turns are permitted

☐   only for emergency use

☐   only stopping

☐   only parking is available

Question 28 - Mock Exam

Highway hypnosis, a state of tiredness or unawareness, can occur while driving on the expressway. You can avoid this condition by doing the following:

☐   You're constantly on the phone

☐   listening to really loud music

☐   Frequently changing lanes

☐   Frequently adjust your gaze

Question 29 - Mock Exam

If a driver is under the influence of _____, the chance of an accident increases.

☐   a cup of tea

☐   soft music is being played

☐   alcoholic beverages, illegal substances, or prescription meds

☐   a cup of coffee

Question 30 - Mock Exam

Which way should you aim your front wheels while waiting for oncoming traffic to clear before making a left turn?

☐ Right

☐ Left

☐ In any direction

☐ Straight

Question 31 - Mock Exam

This symbol is used

☐ to make it illegal for vehicles to make a U-turn

☐ to permit vehicles in specific lanes

☐ to forbid vehicles from entering a roadway

☐ to forbid large trucks from entering a route

Question 32 - Mock Exam

Which of the following is a symptom of road rage?

☐ Unnecessarily blowing the horn

☐ Tailgating

☐ Forcing a car off the road

☐ Everything mentioned above

Question 33 - Mock Exam

What is the proper hand signal for making a left turn?

- ☐   Extended hand and arm downward
- ☐   Outwardly extended hand and arm
- ☐   Backwards-extended hand and arm
- ☐   Arm and hand extended upward

Question 34 - Mock Exam

If you are going slower than other traffic on an expressway or motorway, stay in the lane

- ☐   closest to the road's center
- ☐   closest to the road's left side
- ☐   the furthest away from the road's shoulder
- ☐   closest to the road's right side

Question 35 - Mock Exam

Headrests should be set so that the back of the head restraint makes contact with the head restraint. This avoids

- ☐   seat belt tightening during an accident
- ☐   neck injuries which occurs when you are hit from behind
- ☐   occurrences from behind
- ☐   physical harm in a head-on collision

Question 36 - Mock Exam

To designate the edge of a limited-access roadway, mile markers are set along the outside shoulder. They provide information to drivers concerning

    ☐   the speed limits posted on the roadway

    ☐   highways to come

    ☐   the state of the highway

    ☐   their highway locations

Question 37 - Mock Exam

When getting ready to exit a parallel parking place, you should

    ☐   take a look behind you

    ☐   examine your reflections

    ☐   convey your objective by signaling

    ☐   complete all of the preceding tasks

Question 38 - Mock Exam

What should you do if you are one of the first people to arrive at a collision scene?

    ☐   Notify the Police authorities

    ☐   Remove your vehicle from the heavily frequented section of the road

    ☐   Stop. Get medical attention for the injured

    ☐   Carry out all of the preceding steps

Question 39 - Mock Exam

What are the conditions in which you should not pass if you see both a solid and a broken yellow line between opposing lanes of traffic.

☐ If the broken yellow line is on your side

☐ On both sides

☐ Of the solid yellow line is not on your side

☐ If the solid yellow line is on your side

Question 40 - Mock Exam

What does this sign mean?

☐ A one-way street awaits

☐ The divided carriageway comes to an end ahead

☐ Traffic is congealing ahead

☐ A divided highway begins ahead of you

Question 41 - Mock Exam

If you are turning left, you must begin the turn

☐ on the far-right lane

☐ at the crossroads

☐ in the middle lane

☐ on the far-left lane

Parking places for people with disabilities are denoted by

☐   pavement markings in white

☐   pavement marks in red

☐   pavement marks in blue

☐   pavement markings in yellow

Question 43 - Mock Exam

Which of the following turning rules is incorrect?

☐   When making a turn, stay in the proper lane throughout the turn

☐   Where there are no turn signals, you must choose the lane that is the furthest away from where you came from

☐   When making a left turn, try not to cut the corner too harshly

☐   Avoid swinging wide to the left when performing a right turn

Question 44 - Mock Exam

A center lane with a solid and a broken yellow line on each side is for _____ and can be used by vehicles driving in either direction.

☐   passing

☐   left turns

☐   right turns

☐   all of the above

Question 45 - Mock Exam

Which of the following blind spot statements is incorrect?

☐ Your vehicle has blind spots in the left and right rear corners

☐ Blind spots are smaller in larger automobiles

☐ Avoid driving in the blind spot of another driver

☐ Look over your shoulders to compensate for blind spots

Question 46 - Mock Exam

Partially hydroplaning can occur in a common passenger car at speeds as low as

☐ 45 mph

☐ 55 mph

☐ 65 mph

☐ 35 mph

Question 47 - Mock Exam

You've arrived at an intersection to take a left on a green arrow signal. The arrow indication then turns yellow. So, what should you do now?

☐ Take a left

☐ Stop

☐ Make a U turn

☐ Reduce your speed

You should _____ on steep downhills to keep your speed under control.

☐   continue to press the brakes

☐   change to a lower gear

☐   firmly press the accelerator

☐   change to a higher gear

Question 49 - Mock Exam

If an emergency vehicle approaches you with its siren and flashing lights activated, you must

☐   immediately stop, wherever you are

☐   continue to move at the same rate

☐   increase your speed and get out of the lane

☐   pull over to the side of the road closest to you

Question 50 - Mock Exam

When making a left turn at a controlled intersection (one with signs or signals), you must yield to

☐   right-hand drive vehicles

☐   oncoming traffic

☐   vehicles following you

☐   cars making a right turn

BONUSES

THE TOP 100 MOST FREQUENTLY ASKED QUESTIONS

Download the top 100 most frequently asked questions. We suggest you revise this document before your exam, so you can be fully prepared! Remember, the more you practice, the better you'll perform on the real DMV exam.

Type in your browser the following link or scan the QR Code

- https://dl.bookfunnel.com/lhf68zpx12

ANSWER SHEETS

DIAGNOSTIC TEST

Question 1 - Diagnostic Test

(B) If you are convicted of reckless driving for the first time, you will face a fine ranging from $25 to $500, up to 90 days in jail, or both. In addition, four points will be added to your driving record. The penalty for a second violation may be severe. [FL Stat 316], [Point System, 9. Your Driving Privilege, Official Florida Driver's Handbook] .192]

Question 2 - Diagnostic Test

(A) Do not obstruct a junction. You must proceed if you have already entered the junction when the green light or green arrow turns yellow or red. Clear the junction by performing the motion you planned.

Question 3 - Diagnostic Test

(D) This is an item marker sign, which is used to alert drivers about things in the road or extremely close to the road's edge. The stripes point down the road, toward the safe side. This sign advises that you should continue to the right in order to pass the object.

Question 4 - Diagnostic Test

(C) If you are guilty of passing a stopped school bus with its red lights flashing, you will be fined at least $100 and will have four points added to your driving record. [FL Stat 316.172], [FL Stat 318.18],

[Point System, 9. Your Driving Privilege, Official Florida Driver's Handbook].

Question 5 - Diagnostic Test

(A) Sequential arrow panels can be employed in work zones 24 hours a day, seven days a week. This one indicates that the lane ahead is closed and that you should take the lane to your left.

Question 6 - Diagnostic Test

(A) This sign indicates that you are not permitted to park on the left side of the sign at any time.

Question 7 - Diagnostic Test

(C) Bicycles must be ridden towards the right edge of the road on most roads. On a one-way street with at least two lanes, however, you may also ride on the left side of the road. [Florida Statute 316] .2065]

Question 8 - Diagnostic Test

(C) When a vehicle is making or about to make a left turn, you may pass on the right. When there are two or more lanes of traffic traveling in the same direction as you, you may also pass on the right. (This might apply to a multilane motorway or a one-way street.)

Question 9 - Diagnostic Test

(D) This sign indicates that a rest spot is available on the right.

Question 10 - Diagnostic Test

(A) This sign warns that there will be a double curve ahead. The road ahead bends to the right, then to the left. (A winding road sign would be posted instead if there was a triple curve coming.) Slow down, stay to the right, and do not pass.

Question 11 - Diagnostic Test

(A) Many roadways have a solid white line indicating the right edge. This line denotes the roadway's outer edge and may only be crossed by cars traveling to or from the shoulder. A yellow line delineates the left edge.

Question 12 - Diagnostic Test

(B) This sign warns that there will be a double curve ahead. The road ahead bends to the right, then to the left. (A winding road sign would be posted instead if there was a triple curve coming.) Slow down, stay to the right, and do not pass.

Question 13 - Diagnostic Test

(C) Unlike in many other states, you can make the same types of turns at a steady red arrow as you can with a steady red light in Florida. That is, you may turn right at a red arrow pointing right; you may turn left at a red arrow pointing left, but only from one one-way street to another one-way street. Before turning, you must still come to a complete stop and yield to oncoming vehicles and pedestrians.

Question 14 - Diagnostic Test

(A) This sign indicates that U-turns are not permitted in this area.

Question 15 - Diagnostic Test

(C) This is a sign for a freeway intersection. This sign alerts you to the fact that you are approaching an interchange.

PRACTICE TEST 1

Question 1 - Practice Test 1
(C) Yellow lines are also utilized as left-edge lines on one-way streets.

Question 2 - Practice Test 1
(D) When you drive too fast on a wet road, you may experience hydroplaning. If your vehicle begins to hydroplane, do not apply the brakes. Braking too hard may cause your vehicle to slip out of control. Instead, remove your foot from the accelerator and allow your car to slow down until hydroplaning ceases.

Question 3 - Practice Test 1
(A) For entering freeways, entrance ramps are provided. Typically, the entrance ramp leads to an acceleration lane. Increase your speed as you approach and enter the acceleration lane to match the vehicles in the through lanes. Keep an eye out for an opening in freeway traffic, activate your turn signal and merge smoothly with the rest of the traffic. Unless absolutely necessary, do not stop or slow down in the acceleration lane.

Question 4 - Practice Test 1
(D) Vehicles approaching from a private road or driveway must come to a complete stop and yield to vehicles on public roads.

Question 5 - Practice Test 1
(C) When you wear a lap and shoulder belt together, your chances of getting seriously wounded in a crash are considerably reduced. The lap belt covers your lower body and prevents ejection from the car. Your head and chest are protected by the shoulder belt from colliding with the dashboard or windshield.

Question 6 - Practice Test 1
(A) Turn on your low-beam headlights to improve visibility in fog, rain or snow. High beams can produce glare by reflecting off precipitation.

Question 7 - Practice Test 1
(A) When (1) the vehicle is making or about to make a left turn, or (2) there are two or more lanes of traffic traveling in the same direction as you, you may pass on the right. (On a multilane highway or a one-way street, this could be the case.)

Question 8 - Practice Test 1
(D) According to statistics, 30 percent of traffic fatalities are caused by striking the steering assembly, while another 40 percent are caused by impacting the windshield, windshield frame or instrument panel. Wearing a lap/shoulder belt significantly minimizes your chances of being killed in a crash. The lap belt covers your lower body and prevents ejection. The shoulder belt prevents your head and chest from colliding with the steering column or windshield.

Question 9 - Practice Test 1
(D) Don't stop, back up or try to turn around if you miss your exit on a

freeway. This greatly increases the possibility of a collision. Instead, proceed to the next exit and find a way to return from there.

Question 10 - Practice Test 1
(A) The driver of the vehicle on the left must yield to the driver of the vehicle on the right, when two cars enter an uncontrolled intersection (one that is not regulated by signs or signals) from different highways, at roughly the same time.

Question 11 - Practice Test 1
(B) At intersections and crosswalks, you must yield the right-of-way to pedestrians.

Question 12 - Practice Test 1
(C) You must get clear of any intersection, pull over to the curb or side of the road and come to a complete stop if an emergency vehicle with flashing red or blue lights and a siren approaches from either direction.

Question 13 - Practice Test 1
(D) Bicycles must abide by the same traffic laws as other vehicles. When approaching an uncontrolled intersection (one without traffic signs or signals), yield to the vehicle or bicycle that arrives first. If other vehicles or bicycles arrive around the same time, you must yield to the one on your right.

Question 14 - Practice Test 1
(A) Do not spend time in a no-zone. No-Zones are wide regions around trucks, buses and other large vehicles where cars may disappear into blind spots or get too close to prevent the truck driver from properly stopping or maneuvering. To the front, back and sides of the vehicle, there are no-zones. It is impossible to totally avoid the no-zones created by a heavy truck. However, do not stay in a no-zone for any longer than is necessary to pass the vehicle safely and never tailgate a truck.

Question 15 - Practice Test 1
(B) When the road is wet, worn or bald tires can increase stopping distance and make turning more difficult. Unbalanced tires or low tire pressures can result in faster tire wear and reduced fuel economy, as well as, making the vehicle more difficult to steer and stop.

Question 16 - Practice Test 1
(D) For entering freeways, entrance ramps are available. Typically, the entrance ramp leads to an acceleration lane. Increase your speed to match that of the vehicles in the through lanes as you approach and enter the acceleration lane. Keep an eye out for a gap in the motorway traffic, engage your turn signal and join gently with the other vehicles. If it's not absolutely required, don't stop or slow down in the acceleration lane.

Question 17 - Practice Test 1
(A) If you intend to turn beyond an intersection, wait until you are within the intersection to signal (drivers in the intersection may pull into your path). Another car may believe you

want to turn at the intersection if you signal before entering the intersection.

Question 18 - Practice Test 1

(B) If the street is too narrow to make a U-turn, you can turn around by making a three-point turn, unless it is prohibited.

Question 19 - Practice Test 1

(A) A motorcycle, like other motor vehicles, requires the entire lane width to drive safely. Even if the road is wide and the motorcycle is riding to one side, never drive alongside a motorcycle in the same lane.

Question 20 - Practice Test 1

(D) Do not attempt to swerve back onto the pavement if your vehicle's wheels have drifted onto the shoulder of the road. This may cause the vehicle to become unbalanced. Instead, slow down and stay on the shoulder, then gently, return to the road.

Question 21 - Practice Test 1

(B) Apply the brakes carefully while stopping on packed snow or ice. Braking hard on a car without anti-lock brakes (ABS) might lock the wheels and cause a skid. Pump the brakes instead. Begin by slamming on the brakes. If your wheels freeze up, let go of the brakes to get them moving again, then squeeze them down again. Continue pumping until the vehicle comes to a halt. Note: If your vehicle has anti-lock brakes, do not attempt this. ABS will pump the brakes on its own to keep the wheels

from locking, allowing you to press the brake pedal firmly until the car comes to a complete stop. You can disengage the ABS by pumping the brakes.

Question 22 - Practice Test 1

(C) If you wish to make a turn, make sure other vehicles are aware of your intentions. Continue to give signals until you're ready to make the actual turn. Hand and arm extended outward is the proper hand signal for a left turn.

Question 23 - Practice Test 1

(A) Defensive driving, according to the National Safety Council, is 'driving to save lives, time and money, regardless of the conditions around you or the conduct of others'. Defensive driving is anticipating potentially harmful scenarios, such as road conditions and other people's mistakes and devising a strategy for dealing with them. To be a defensive driver, you must be aware of what is going on around you. You must keep your eyes on the road ahead, to the sides and behind you. You owe it to yourself to learn how to drive defensively.

Question 24 - Practice Test 1

(D) Parking places for people with impairments are marked with blue pavement markings.

Question 25 - Practice Test 1

(B) If you are stopped at an intersection and another vehicle is approaching from behind at high speed, you should move slightly forward (but not into the intersection) to give the approaching vehicle more room to stop.

Question 26 - Practice Test 1
(C) If at all feasible, park in a designated space. If you have to park on the road, try to park as far away from the traffic as possible. If a curb exists, park as close to it as possible.

Question 27 - Practice Test 1
(B) If your vehicle's turn signals have failed, you must employ hand and arm signals. The hand and arm are bent at 90 degrees and pointing upward to signify a right turn. The hand and arm are stretched leftward to indicate a left turn. The hand and arm are bent at 90 degrees and pointing downward to slow or stop.

Question 28 - Practice Test 1
(A) Airbags are dangerous for small children. Children under the age of 12 should never ride in the front seat of an airbag-equipped vehicle unless the passenger airbag is first deactivated.

Question 29 - Practice Test 1
(D) If you are one of the first people to arrive at a collision scene, the first thing you should do is pull your vehicle off the road. Then, turn off the ignition of any vehicles involved in the accident. If there is no danger of fire, do not move injured people. Notify emergency personnel and avoid standing in traffic lanes.

Inquire of those who have stopped to warn oncoming traffic.

Question 30 - Practice Test 1
(B) High-speed traffic is handled securely on freeways and interstate routes. When approaching or departing a motorway, do not cross a solid line.

Question 31 - Practice Test 1
(D) When three or more lanes are traveling in the same direction, the center lanes usually provide the smoothest traffic flow. Drivers that want to travel quicker or pass should use the left lane. The right lane should be used by slower cars and those exiting the highway.

Question 32 - Practice Test 1
(A) When a vehicle turns, the back wheels travel a lesser distance than the front wheels. The larger the difference, the longer the vehicle is. Before turning, a tractor-trailer may swing out. Don't try to pass a tractor-trailer on the right if you notice it moving left, the truck may be preparing to turn right. Examine the turn signals.

Question 33 - Practice Test 1
(C) Car and motorcycle collisions are most likely to occur at intersections. The automobile driver, in most cases, fails to detect the motorcycle and turns across its path.

Question 34 - Practice Test 1
(B) Crosswalk lines are two white or longitudinal lines that indicate where

pedestrians may walk. Do not use your vehicle to obstruct a crosswalk. Always yield to pedestrians in crosswalks, whether marked or unmarked.

Question 35 - Practice Test 1

(B) In highway and street maintenance zones, flag persons (flaggers) are frequently stationed to safely stop, delay or guide traffic through these areas. Flaggers wear orange vests, shirts or jackets and direct traffic through work zones with red or orange flags or STOP/SLOW paddles.

Question 36 - Practice Test 1

(B) Even if there are alternative lanes available, you must not pass a vehicle ahead of you that has stopped for a pedestrian. Pedestrians are frequently exposed to this danger. Instead, come to a complete stop and wait for the pedestrian to cross at least half of the road.

Question 37 - Practice Test 1

(C) When slowing or stopping, you must either use the brake-operated signal lights or a hand signal to alert the driver behind you.

Question 38 - Practice Test 1

(C) If you begin to skid, be calm, take your foot off the throttle, gently slow your vehicle down and carefully steer in the direction you want the front of your vehicle to go. In other words, if your vehicle's rear end skids left, steer left. if your vehicle's rear end skids right, steer right.

Avoid braking, particularly if your vehicle has an antilock braking system (ABS). The vehicle may overshoot and begin to slide in the opposite direction. To avoid this, turn your vehicle in the opposite direction, as soon as it begins to straighten out. This technique, known as 'driving into the skid', will align the back and front of your car.

Question 39 - Practice Test 1

(B) An intersection is a road junction at which two or more roads cross or merge. There are three types of intersections: controlled, uncontrolled and blind. An interchange is a road junction where two or more roads cross over each other (at different levels) so that traffic flow is not impeded. There are interchanges such as diamond, cloverleaf and stack.

Question 40 - Practice Test 1

(A) Make sure to keep the steering wheel straight while you tilt your head to look for blind areas. The natural propensity for people is to turn their arms in the same direction as their heads.

PRACTICE TEST 2

Question 1 - Practice Test 2

(C) Unlike in many other states, you can make the same types of turns at a steady red arrow as you can at a steady red light in Florida. That is, you may turn right at a red arrow pointing right; you may turn left at a red arrow pointing left, but only from one one-way street to another one-way street. Before turning, you must still come to a complete stop and yield to oncoming vehicles and pedestrians.

Question 2 - Practice Test 2

(D) You should maintain a following distance of at least three to four seconds behind the car ahead of you during your driving skills test. Even if you can't see any pedestrians or other vehicles, signal whenever you intend to turn or change lanes. Maintain good posture by keeping both hands on the steering wheel and not resting your elbow on the window.

Question 3 - Practice Test 2

(B) You may cross a broken yellow line on your side of the center dash stripe to pass if it is safe to do so.

Question 4 - Practice Test 2

(C) If at all feasible, park in a designated space. If you must park on the road, park as far away from traffic as possible. If there is a curb, try to park as near to it as possible.

Question 5 - Practice Test 2

(D) Allow another car passing you on the left to pass safely and do not raise your speed.

Question 6 - Practice Test 2

(D) When a car ahead of you stops for a pedestrian, even if there are two lanes open, you must not pass the stopped vehicle. For pedestrians, this is a common hazard.

Question 7 - Practice Test 2

(B) If a car approaches from the left with its turn signal on while you are waiting at a stop sign to turn right, do not attempt to turn until the other vehicle has actually begun to turn. Then and only then should you begin your turn. Drivers are prone to making mistakes or changing their minds. The driver of the other car may, at the last second, alter his or her mind and opt to proceed straight through the junction. Alternatively, the driver of the other car may have inadvertently activated the turn signal and is intending to proceed straight through the junction. You risk colliding with the other car if you rely on it turning as its turn signal indicates. Always be on the lookout for faulty signals and bad drivers.

Question 8 - Practice Test 2

(A) When a vehicle is making or about to make a left turn, you may pass on the right. When there are two or more lanes of traffic traveling in the same direction as you, you may also pass on the right. (This might apply to a multilane motorway or a one-way street.)

Question 9 - Practice Test 2

(D) If the lights flash or the gates are lowered at a crossing designated with automatic flasher units or automatic crossing gates, you must stop and remain stopped until the lights stop flashing and the gates are raised. At crossings with merely a stop sign, you must halt and then advance only when you establish that no train or pedestrians are approaching and that it is safe to cross.

Question 10 - Practice Test 2

(A) This is a regulation sign instructing you to continue straight or make a right turn.

Question 11 - Practice Test 2

(D) When overtaking and passing another car on a two-lane road, pass exclusively on the vehicle's left side.

Question 12 - Practice Test 2

(D) Intersections that are not protected by stop signs, yield signs, or traffic lights are referred to as open intersections. To establish which vehicles can advance first at an open crossroads, follow the right-of-way laws.

Question 13 - Practice Test 2

(C) If there are no warning devices or merely a crossbuck sign at a railroad grade crossing, slow down and look and listen for a train before proceeding. Any approaching train must be given the right-of-way.

Question 14 - Practice Test 2

(A) Car and motorcycle collisions are most likely to occur at intersections. Typically, the automobile driver fails to see the motorcycle and turns into the path of the motorcycle.

Question 15 - Practice Test 2

(A) Regulatory devices direct you to halt, move in a specific direction, or slow down. All regulatory devices indicate the measures that you, the driver, must do. Failure to comply may result in sanctions.

Question 16 - Practice Test 2

(D) If you detect a car approaching you in your lane, hit the brakes hard, sound your horn, flash your headlights, and veer to the right as far as you safely can. Try not to swerve to the left. The other car may abruptly recover and re-enter that lane, resulting in a head-on collision. Accidents involving a head-on collision are frequently fatal.

Question 17 - Practice Test 2

(A) When traveling in wide terrain with no traffic in sight, you should utilize high beams. High lights allow you to see further ahead, but they can also blind the driver of another car. When you are within 500 feet of an oncoming vehicle or within 300 feet of a vehicle you are following, Florida law requires you to dim your headlights. Glare can also be caused by high beams reflecting off precipitation. In the event of fog, rain, or snow, use low beams.

Question 18 - Practice Test 2

(B) Allow space for vehicles entering the expressway if you are in the right lane. As much as feasible, the right lane should be kept free for traffic approaching or exiting the highway.

Question 19 - Practice Test 2

(A) This sign denotes a service. It signifies that telephone service is available in the near future.

Question 20 - Practice Test 2

(A) To control traffic, vertical rectangular signs with black characters on a white background are employed. Some examples include speed limit signs and lane control signs.

Question 21 - Practice Test 2

(A) This work zone sign indicates that there will be a flagger ahead. Flaggers are frequently found in highway or street construction zones. They wear orange vests, shirts, or jackets and utilize red flags or STOP/SLOW paddles to direct traffic through these locations safely. You must obey the flagger's instructions.

Question 22 - Practice Test 2

(A) A double solid yellow line denotes the middle of a road and separates opposing traffic lanes.

Passing is prohibited on both sides of the line. You may only cross the line to perform a left turn.

Question 23 - Practice Test 2

(C) A reflective triangle orange insignia on the back of a vehicle identifies it as a slow-moving vehicle, which Florida defines as a four-wheeled vehicle with a top speed of more than 20 mph but less than 25 mph. Farm trucks and road maintenance vehicles are examples of slow-moving vehicles. Slow down and proceed with caution if you come across one of these cars. Keep your cool; the car may pull over to let you through. [Florida Statute 320] .01]

Question 24 - Practice Test 2

(D) If an emergency vehicle with a siren or flashing lights is immediately behind you in heavy traffic, maintain driving slowly until you can move out of the way.

Question 25 - Practice Test 2

(D) You must present proof of Personal Injury Protection (PIP) and Property Damage Liability (PDL) insurance coverage before you can register your car in Florida. If a police officer pulls you over for a traffic violation or an equipment check, he or she may request your driver's license, proof of insurance, or car registration. You must have this evidence of insurance with you at all times when driving.

Question 26 - Practice Test 2

(A) This sign tells you that the one-way street you're on is about to become a two-way split street. Keep to the right and keep an eye out for oncoming vehicles.

Question 27 - Practice Test 2

(B) Slow down, move into the right lane if possible, and encourage the driver behind you to pass. If this fails, pull over, come to a complete stop, and allow the tailgater pass. Don't try to outrun or outpace the tailgater by increasing your speed. Some tailgaters believe that no speed is too fast.

Question 28 - Practice Test 2

(D) If traffic from another road is merging onto the road you're on, reduce your speed and alter your vehicle position to allow the vehicles to join safely.

Question 29 - Practice Test 2

(C) It is illegal in Florida to drive off the pavement or a heavily used area of the road to pass another vehicle on the right. [Florida Statute 316] .084]

Question 30 - Practice Test 2

(C) If there is a broken line (white or yellow) next to your lane, you may pass another car.

Question 31 - Practice Test 2

(D) When a traffic signal at an intersection turns green, make sure the path is clear of any other cars that may still be in or approaching the intersection. Yield to any remaining pedestrians on the road.

The majority of traffic accidents occur within the first few seconds after the light has changed.

Question 32 - Practice Test 2

(D) Your brake lights signal to other drivers that you are slowing down. If you plan to stop or slow down in an unexpected location, notify others behind you by quickly pressing your brake pedal three or four times to flash your brake lights.

Question 33 - Practice Test 2

(A) If your engine quits while driving around a bend, grab the steering wheel with both hands and steer to the right side of the road. (If your vehicle has power steering, a loss of engine power will result in a loss of power assist, requiring you to apply greater force to the steering wheel.) Bring your vehicle to a halt. (If your vehicle has power brakes, a lack of engine power will result in a loss of power assist, requiring you to push the brake pedal extra hard.) Shift into park (if you have an automatic transmission) or neutral (if you have a manual transmission) and try to restart the engine.

Question 34 - Practice Test 2

(C) Keep plenty of space between your vehicle and other vehicles on all sides to assist avoid an accident.

Question 35 - Practice Test 2

(A) If you find yourself losing control of the steering wheel, take your foot off the gas pedal. Turn on your emergency flashers and allow your car to come to a complete stop. To keep your vehicle from spinning, apply the brakes softly.

Question 36 - Practice Test 2

(A) When exiting an acceleration lane and entering an interstate highway, you must keep up with other vehicles or respect posted speed limits.

Question 37 - Practice Test 2

(A) This sign denotes the presence of a Y-intersection ahead. The road ahead divides into two routes. Be prepared to turn in one direction or the other if traffic crosses your path.

Question 38 - Practice Test 2

(C) If an incoming car has its high-beam headlights turned on, avoid staring at the lights. To avoid being briefly blinded, keep your gaze on the right side of the road.

Question 39 - Practice Test 2

(B) When two or more vehicles arrive at a four-way stop at different times, the first to stop should be the first to go. When two vehicles traveling on different roads come at a four-way stop about the same time, the vehicle on the left must yield to the vehicle on the right.

Question 40 - Practice Test 2

(D) A persistent yellow traffic light indicates that the light will soon turn red. If you can do so safely, you should stop. (Never try to "race the light" by speeding up before it turns red.) But don't come to a quick halt and risk skidding or being rear-ended by the vehicle in front of you. If you are unable to safely stop, proceed with caution into the junction.

ROAD SIGNS

Question 1 - Road Signals Full
(A) This is a forewarning sign that may be placed ahead of the railroad crossing. Vehicles must slow down, look, listen and be prepared to come to a complete stop at the crossing ahead.

Question 2 - Road Signs
(A) Sequential arrow panels can be used in work zones 24 hours a day, seven days a week. This one indicates that the lane ahead is closed and that you should take the lane to your left.

Question 3 - Road Signs
(B) Route marker signs indicate the type of road you're on as well as the specific road you're on. Highway marker signs are typically shield-shaped and Interstate shield signs are colored red, white and blue. This sign denotes that you are on Interstate Highway 22. (I-22 for short). I-22 connects Mississippi's I-269 to Alabama's I-65.

Question 4 - Road Signs
(C) These are lane guidance signs. Vehicles on the left must turn left, while vehicles on the right may either continue straight or turn right.

Question 5 - Road Signs
(B) Traffic moving in opposite directions is separated by yellow lines. On two-way streets, there will be either a double solid yellow line or a solid yellow line next to a broken yellow line.

Question 6 - Road Signs
(C) This sign indicates that the divided highway is coming to an end. The road will be converted to a two-way street. Keep to the right and keep an eye out for oncoming traffic.

Question 7 - Road Signs
(B) This sign is typically displayed at an intersection with a combination of signals, including a green arrow pointing left. When the green arrow is illuminated, you may make a protected left turn. Oncoming traffic will be stopped at a red light. This sign indicates that if the green arrow disappears and a steady green light appears, you may still make a left turn, but you must now yield to oncoming traffic, before turning.

Question 8 - Road Signs
(D) This sign indicates that traffic in the right lane must turn right, while traffic in the second lane may either continue straight or turn right.

Question 9 - Road Signs
(B) A disabled crossing is indicated by the sign ahead. Slow down and take your time.

Question 10 - Road Signs
(D) This is a red flag. Bicyclists and pedestrians frequently cross the road in the vicinity of the sign. You must drive cautiously and be prepared to stop.

Question 11 - Road Signs
(B) This railroad crossing signal features a bell and flashing red

lights to alert drivers that a train is approaching. When the bell rings and the lights flash, come to a halt.

Question 12 - Road Signs
(A) When the road ahead is clear, this image indicates that passing on the left is permitted. Due to oncoming traffic, overtaking and passing should be done with caution.

Question 13 - Road Signs
(D) This sign indicates that a rest area is available on the right.

Question 14 - Road Signs
(C) This is a warning sign indicating the presence of a playground ahead.

Question 15 - Road Signs
(A) This sign denotes a service. It denotes a rest stop one mile ahead.

Question 16 - Road Signs
(A) This sign warns drivers that a nearby side road crosses a railroad track. When turning onto the side road, proceed with caution.

Question 17 - Road Signs
(C) This sign indicates that you are not permitted to park in a handicap zone unless you have the necessary permit.

Question 18 - Road Signs
(C) A vehicle with a reflective triangular orange emblem on the rear identifies it as a low-speed or slow-moving vehicle, which is typically defined as a motor vehicle with a top speed of no more than 25 mph. Farm vehicles and road maintenance vehicles are examples of slow-moving vehicles. Slow down and proceed with caution if you come across one of these vehicles.

Question 19 - Road Signs
(B) Blue-and-white signs direct you to services such as gas stations, fast-food restaurants, motels and hospitals. The sign in picture B indicates that there is a hospital ahead.

Question 20 - Road Signs
(C) The larger sign alerts you to the impending arrival of a speed zone. The speed limit is indicated by the smaller sign. The speed limit will be reduced to 45 mph ahead in this case. Prepare to slow down so that you don't go over the speed limit.

Question 21 - Road Signs
(A) Vertical rectangular signs typically provide instructions or inform you of traffic laws. Motorists, pedestrians and cyclists are given instructions by such regulatory signs.

Question 22 - Road Signs
(C) This sign indicates that the road ahead curves in the direction indicated by the arrow.

Question 23 - Road Signs
(B) This sign indicates a bicycle crossing. This sign forewarns you that a bikeway will cross the road ahead.

Question 24 - Road Signs

(C) If you see this sign while driving in the left lane, turn left at the next intersection.

Question 25 - Road Signs
(D) This sign indicates that there will be a double curve ahead. The road ahead bends to the right, then to the left. (A winding road sign would be posted instead if there was a triple curve ahead.) Slow down, stay to the right and do not pass.

Question 26 - Road Signs
(D) Pedestrian signals are only used to direct pedestrian traffic. This pedestrian signal indicates that pedestrians may enter the crosswalk to cross the road. (Older signals displayed the word 'WALK' instead.) A signal with an upraised hand warns pedestrians not to enter the crosswalk. (Older signals displayed the words 'DO NOT WALK' instead.)

Question 27 - Road Signs
(A) This is a navigational sign. This sign indicates the presence of a hospital ahead.

Question 28 - Road Signs
(D) You must follow the broken yellow centerline to the right. When it is safe to do so, you may cross this line, to pass another vehicle or turn.

Question 29 - Road Signs
(A) This sign indicates an exit number. This is the number assigned to a highway exit at a junction. If an interchange has more than one exit, a letter may be added to indicate which exit it is: 117A, 117B and so on.

Question 30 - Road Signs
(A) This is a service sign directing you to a gas station.

Question 31 - Road Signs
(B) This sign warns that the road ahead will be divided into a divided highway. A divider, also known as a median, will be used to separate opposing lanes. Continue to the right.

Question 32 - Road Signs
(A) Travelers can get important information from dynamic message signs. Messages can be changed to reflect current weather conditions, route traffic, construction schedules, incidents and so on.

Question 33 - Road Signs
(B) If you see this sign, it means you're driving in the wrong direction. Make a U-turn.

Question 34 - Road Signs
(D) This sign indicates that the maximum nighttime speed limit is 45 mph.

Question 35 - Road Signs
(A) This is a warning sign for emergency vehicles. It denotes that emergency vehicles from fire stations or other emergency facilities may enter the roadway. When an emergency vehicle approaches from any direction, you must yield to it if it is sounding a

siren, blowing an air horn or flashing lights.

Question 36 - Road Signs

(D) This sign may be found at the end of some T-intersections. It means that you must yield the right of way or come to a complete stop, before turning right or left onto the through road.

Question 37 - Road Signs

(C) The middle lane is a two-way left-turn lane, also known as a shared center turning lane, according to the sign and pavement markings. Vehicles coming from either direction may enter this lane only to turn left. This lane must not be used for through traffic at any time.

Question 38 - Road Signs

(C) This sign indicates that U-turns are not permitted in this area.

Question 39 - Road Signs

(B) This sign denotes a T-junction. This sign indicates that the road you're on is about to come to an end. Prepare to make a right or left turn. Yield to oncoming traffic.

Question 40 - Road Signs

(C) At a roundabout, this is a speed advisory sign. In the roundabout, the speed limit is 15 mph.

Question 41 - Road Signs

(D) This is a traffic control sign. This sign indicates that traffic must only make a left turn.

Question 42 - Road Signs

(A) The arrow represents a turn to the right. A red slash inside a red circle, on the other hand, means 'no'. This regulatory sign forbids drivers from turning right. This sign is usually found on the right side of the road or above a travel lane.

Question 43 - Road Signs

(B) This sign denotes a service. It indicates that telephone service is available and within proximity.

Question 44 - Road Signs

(B) This sign is located next to a route marker sign. It means you'll have to turn right soon to enter or continue on that route.

Question 45 - Road Signs

(B) This sign indicates the maximum safe speed for entering or exiting an expressway. Slow down to the indicated speed (in this case, 30 mph).

(B) Question 46 - Road Signs

A two-lane, two-way road may have a single broken (dashed) yellow line. If it is safe to do so, vehicles on either side may pass.

Question 47 - Road Signs

(C) This regulatory sign indicates a complete halt. At a stop sign, you must come to a complete stop before the stop line, crosswalk or intersection, whichever comes first. After that, yield to pedestrians and other vehicles and proceed only when the intersection is clear. You must come to a complete stop near the sign and yield the right-of-way to other vehicles.

Question 48 - Road Signs
(D) Lane use control signs are rectangular, black-and-white signs that indicate, whether or not, turning is required from specified lanes at an intersection. You must only drive in the direction indicated for your traffic lane.

Question 49 - Road Signs
(B) This sign indicates the presence of a four-way intersection ahead. Cross-traffic entering the roadway should be avoided by drivers.

Question 50 - Road Signs
(A) No is represented by a red circle with a diagonal red slash. The red slash across the truck denotes that trucks are not permitted on this road. Truck drivers must seek alternate routes.

Question 51 - Road Signs
(A) This sign denotes a railroad crossing with low ground clearance. The railroad crossing is elevated to the point where a vehicle with a long wheelbase or low ground clearance can become stuck on the tracks. This type of railroad crossing should not be a problem for a car driver unless he or she is towing a trailer or driving a motorhome with low ground clearance.

Question 52 - Road Signs
(B) If there is a broken or dashed line (white or yellow) next to your lane, you may pass if it is safe to do so.

Question 53 - Road Signs
(C) A stop sign is a white-on-red eight-sided sign that indicates that other traffic has the right-of-way. Before proceeding, you must always come to a complete stop and yield to oncoming traffic.

Question 54 - Road Signs
(D) Work zone signs alert motorists to unusual or potentially hazardous conditions on or near the traveled route. The letters or symbols on these signs are black on an orange background. Slow down and pay close attention if you see these signs.

Question 55 - Road Signs
(A) Sequencing or large flashing Arrow panels can be used in work zones both during the day and at night, to direct drivers into specific traffic lanes and to notify them that a portion of the road or street ahead is closed.

Question 56 - Road Signs
(A) The arrow's shape indicates that you're about to enter a winding road. There are at least three curves on a winding road. Slow down and take your time.

Question 57 - Road Signs
(C) When the road surface is wet, it becomes slick. This sign is frequently found near bridges and overpasses.

Question 58 - Road Signs

(B) This is a sign for a freeway interchange. This sign alerts you to the fact that you are approaching an interchange.

Question 59 - Road Signs
(C) This sign indicates that you are approaching an overpass, with a clearance of 13 feet 6 inches from the roadway surface to the overpass.

Question 60 - Road Signs
(D) This sign indicates that you are not permitted to park on the left side of the sign at any time.

Question 61 - Road Signs
(A) This is a crossing sign for animals. The animal depicted on the sign (in this case, a deer) is common in this area. Keep an eye out for these animals crossing the road, especially at dawn and dusk. Herds of deer, elk and other wildlife travel in groups. If you see one, keep an eye out for more. A collision with a large animal has the potential to kill the animal, damage your vehicle and even injure a passenger in your vehicle.

Question 62 - Road Signs
(C) When there are children present, this sign warns drivers not to exceed the posted speed limit in a school zone or school crossing. The maximum permissible speed, in this case, is 15 mph.

Question 63 - Road Signs
(B) This is a sign indicating a service. It is recommended that drivers use lodging facilities if necessary.

Question 64 - Road Signs
(A) This white diamond sign indicates that the road is reserved for high-occupancy vehicles (HOVs) from Monday to Friday, at the times specified.

Question 65 - Road Signs
(D) A stop sign accompanied by this sign at an intersection indicates that the intersection is a four-way stop. Each approaching roadway is marked with a stop sign and a '4-Way' sign.

Question 66 - Road Signs
(B) This sign alerts you to the fact that you are about to approach a T-intersection from the terminating roadway. You must turn left or right at the T-intersection after yielding the right-of-way to through traffic if necessary.

Question 67 - Road Signs
(A) This sign directs you to turn right onto Route 47 and head north.

Question 68 - Road Signs
(B) This is a warning sign indicating that you are approaching an airport.

Question 69 - Road Signs
(A) This sign indicates a side road ahead. Keep an eye out for vehicles approaching from that direction.

Question 70 - Road Signs
(B) This sign indicates a sharp left turn. Slow down (to the

recommended speed of 25 mph, in this case), keep right as you turn and do not pass.

Question 71 - Road Signs

(D) A speed limit sign indicates the maximum legal speed permitted on the expressway under ideal driving conditions.

Question 72 - Road Signs

(D) The school zone sign is pentagonal in shape (five sides) and has a yellow or yellow-green background.

Question 73 - Road Signs

(C) This sign warns of a road closure ahead, but there is an alternate route in 1,000 feet.

Question 74 - Road Signs

(B) This sign indicates that there will be a hiccup in the road ahead. To avoid losing control, slow down.

Question 75 - Road Signs

(B) Pedestrian signals are only used to direct pedestrian traffic. This signal with an upraised hand informs pedestrians that they are not permitted to enter the crosswalk to cross the roadway. (Older signals displayed the words 'DO NOT WALK' instead.) Pedestrians may enter the crosswalk if they see a signal depicting a person walking. (Older signals displayed the word 'WALK' instead.)

Question 76 - Road Signs

(A) Yellow lines separate traffic lanes traveling in opposite directions. Except when turning left, do not cross a solid yellow line.

Question 77 - Road Signs

(D) This work zone sign indicates that there will be a flagger (flag person) ahead. Flaggers are frequently found in highway or street construction zones. They wear orange vests, shirts or jackets and use red flags or STOP/SLOW paddles to direct traffic through these areas safely. You must obey the flagger's instructions.

Question 78 - Road Signs

(A) If you see this sign while driving on the main road, be prepared for other cars and trucks to enter your lane.

Question 79 - Road Signs

(A) This is a warning sign indicating the presence of a narrow bridge ahead. The bridge is wide enough for two lanes of traffic, but there is very little clearance.

Question 80 - Road Signs

(B) This type of warning sign alerts drivers ahead of a reduction in the number of lanes. This sign indicates that the right lane is coming to an end ahead. Drivers in the right lane are required to merge to the left. Drivers in the left lane should give way to vehicles in the right lane so that they can merge smoothly.

Question 81 - Road Signs

(C) Consider a flashing red light to be a stop sign. To put it another way, come to a complete stop and then yield the right-of-way before proceeding.

Question 82 - Road Signs
(B) White lines separate traffic lanes moving in the same direction. You must drive between these lane markings.

Question 83 - Road Signs
(C) This sign indicates that workers are performing road maintenance. Slow down, be cautious and obey all signs and instructions. If possible, move into a lane that is further away from the workers.

Question 84 - Road Signs
(A) The majority of warning signs are diamond-shaped and have a yellow background. This sign alerts you to the impending arrival of a stop sign. Prepare to come to a halt and yield. You must come to a complete stop before any stop line or crosswalk, painted on the pavement.

Question 85 - Road Signs
(C) This pentagonal (five-sided) sign indicates that you are approaching a school zone.

Question 86 - Road Signs
(D) A red circle and slash on a prohibitory sign, means 'no'. This sign indicates that left turns are not permitted in this area.

Question 87 - Road Signs
(B) This sign indicates an exit number. These signs direct you to bike paths, parking lots, mile markers and specific exits. You can see how far you are from the exit you want to take, by entering the milepost number and the exit number.

Question 88 - Road Signs
(A) This symbol denotes a soft shoulder. The dirt on the roadside is soft. Except in an emergency, never leave the pavement.

Question 89 - Road Signs
(A) This sign indicates the presence of a traffic island or divider ahead. Keep to the left of this stumbling block.

Question 90 - Road Signs
(A) A red slash within a red circle denotes 'no'. This sign indicates that driving on the railroad tracks is prohibited

Question 91 - Road Signs
(D) A red slash within a red circle denotes 'no'. Pedestrians are not permitted to cross here, according to this regulatory sign.

Question 92 - Road Signs
(A) This is a warning sign indicating a two-way street.

Question 93 - Road Signs
(A) This sign denotes a bicycle lane, which is intended for bicyclists. Cars and trucks should not normally use this lane. Cars and trucks may, however, travel in this lane for a short distance when preparing to turn at the next intersection in many (but not all) states.

Question 94 - Road Signs

(A) This symbol denotes a Y-intersection. The road ahead divides into two directions. Be prepared to turn in one direction or the other, if traffic crosses your path.

Question 95 - Road Signs

(D) Guide signs inform drivers about the type of road they are on, upcoming highway entrances and exits and distances to various destinations. Shield-shaped guide signs are commonly used to identify U.S. Routes and interstate highways. This sign informs you that you are on Interstate 95 (I-95), which runs from Maine to Florida.

Question 96 - Road Signs

(C) The International Symbol of Access for Disabled People is featured on this sign. This means that these parking spaces are only available to people who have disabled parking permits. You must obtain a disabled parking placard or disabled license plates from your state, to park in these spaces.

Question 97 - Road Signs

(B) This sign warns drivers to be on the lookout for cattle crossing the road.

Question 98 - Road Signs

(C) In North America, raising one's hand with the thumb indicates that one wishes to hitch a ride. A red slash within a red circle denotes 'no'. This sign indicates that hitchhiking is prohibited on this stretch of road.

Please do not pick up hitchhikers here.

Question 99 - Road Signs

(D) This is a route marker sign for the United States. A route marker sign's shape and color indicate the type of road you're on. Shield-shaped signs are commonly used to identify U.S. Routes and interstate highways. This sign indicates that you are on US Highway 40. The United States Routes are a network of roads and highways that were built decades before the Interstate Highway System. US Route 40 was built in 1926 and currently connects Silver Summit, UT to Atlantic City, NJ.

Question 100 - Road Signs

(C) This symbol indicates the presence of a pedestrian crosswalk ahead. Pedestrians must be given the right of way by drivers.

Question 101 - Road Signs

(B) This sign indicates that all vehicles are not permitted to pass through this area (buses, trucks, passenger cars, etc.).

Question 102 - Road Signs

(C) A red slash within a red circle denotes 'no'. Bicycles are not permitted on this route, as indicated by this prohibitory sign.

Question 103 - Road Signs

(D) This is an object marker sign, which is used to alert drivers to objects in the road or very close to the road's edge. The stripes point down the road, toward the safe side. This sign indicates that you should continue to the right to pass the object.

Question 104 - Road Signs
(B) Parking is prohibited between 8:30 a.m. and 5:30 p.m., according to this sign.

Question 105 - Road Signs
(A) The road shoulder is much lower than the road surface, as indicated by this sign.

Question 106 - Road Signs
(D) Most states in the United States impose additional penalties for certain traffic violations in work zones under certain conditions, though the conditions and additional penalties vary by state. This sign warns drivers that fines for exceeding the posted speed limit in work zones have been doubled.

Question 107 - Road Signs
(B) This sign warns drivers that there will be a railroad crossing ahead. Drivers must exercise extreme caution.

Question 108 - Road Signs
(A) This sign indicates that there is a speed limit ahead. This is a zone where the speed limit has been reduced. Prepare to slow down so you don't go over the speed limit.

Question 109 - Road Signs
(A) This sign indicates that you may not drive slower than 40 mph under normal traffic, weather and road conditions. These minimum speed limits are in place to improve traffic flow and safety. However, if driving conditions are hazardous, you may drive at a slower speed than the posted minimum.

Question 110 - Road Signs
(A) Lane-use control signals are special overhead signals that allow or disallow the use of specific streets or highway lanes. A continuous red X over a lane indicates that you must not drive in that lane.

Question 111 - Road Signs
(D) This sign indicates that trucks are about to enter or cross the road ahead. Slow down and keep an eye out for trucks.

Question 112 - Road Signs
(A) This sign forewarns of a steep descent ahead. Before you begin the descent, inspect your brakes. Even if your vehicle has an automatic transmission, use low gear to reduce brake wear.

Question 113 - Road Signs
(A) This sign indicates that you are approaching the intersection of your road and U.S. Route 22. The United States Routes are a network of roads and highways that were built decades before the Interstate Highway System. One of the oldest is U.S. Route 22, which connects Cincinnati, Ohio and Newark, New Jersey.

Question 114 - Road Signs

(D) This sign indicates that the vertical clearance on this road is 12'6". (twelve feet six inches). Vehicles taller than this should avoid using this road. Trucks in the United States can legally stand taller than 13 feet.

Question 115 - Road Signs

(A) The sign warns the driver that there will be two-way traffic ahead. Drivers must keep an eye out for traffic coming from the opposite direction.

Question 116 - Road Signs

(C) This is a stop sign. If it is safe to do so, this sign allows you to make a U-turn.

Question 117 - Road Signs

(C) This is a regulatory sign instructing you to continue straight or make a right turn.

Question 118 - Road Signs

(D) This sign indicates that you are not permitted to enter the roadway where the sign is posted.

Question 119 - Road Signs

(D) A diamond-shaped marking indicates that a lane is reserved for specific purposes or vehicles. During rush hour, the lanes are usually reserved for buses or carpool vehicles.

Question 120 - Road Signs

(B) This is a sign with a directional arrow.

Question 121 - Road Signs

(D) This sign indicates that there will be a roundabout ahead. A roundabout is a circular intersection with traffic flowing counterclockwise around a central island. In the roundabout, slow down and prepare to yield to traffic.

Question 122 - Road Signs

(A) This sign forewarns of an impending traffic signal. If the light is yellow or red, prepare to come to a complete stop. These signs are placed on highways with higher speed limits or where your view of the traffic signal ahead may be obstructed.

Question 123 - Road Signs

(C) This warning sign alerts drivers to the possibility of farm equipment crossing the road. Prepare to slow down for slow-moving machinery.

Question 124 - Road Signs

(B) This sign indicates that the road ahead will take a sharp right turn. Slow down and proceed with caution.

Question 125 - Road Signs

(C) At freeway exits and entrance ramps, signs like this one, provide advisory speeds. They display the maximum safe speed to drive at in ideal weather conditions.

Question 126 - Road Signs

(C) This sign indicates that you are not permitted to turn on a red light.

To turn right, you must first wait for a green arrow or green light.

Question 127 - Road Signs

(B) Mileposts are spaced at regular intervals so that drivers are always aware of them. They are installed along the road's edge to provide drivers with information about their location on the highway for navigation and emergency purposes. The distance in miles to the state line or the end of the road is usually indicated by the number on the milepost.

Question 128 - Road Signs

(B) Most public crossings have railroad flashing light signals and crossbuck signs. These signs must be handled in the same manner as a yield sign.

Question 129 - Road Signs

(A) This sign is a nighttime reflector that indicates the location of the road.

Question 130 - Road Signs

(C) Passing is permitted when it can be done safely, as indicated by broken white lines.

Question 131 - Road Signs

(B) During road closures or construction, this sign indicates alternate routes. Pay attention to these cues.

Question 132 - Road Signs

(D) Two lanes traveling in the same direction are separated by a white line. You may cross a broken line to pass or change lanes. You should usually stay in your lane if it's a straight line.

Question 133 - Road Signs

(D) This sign regulates traffic and instructs drivers whether to turn left or straight.

Question 134 - Road Signs

(C) A red slash within a red circle denotes 'no'. This regulatory sign reads 'No Parking'. It is not permitted to park at the sign.

Question 135 - Road Signs

(B) This sign indicates that you must proceed straight. You are unable to turn here.

Question 136 - Road Signs

(C) The center lane is designated for left turns (or U-turns when permitted) and can be used by vehicles traveling in either direction. On the pavement, left-turn arrows for one-way traffic alternate with left-turn arrows for the opposite direction. These lanes are denoted by solid and broken (dashed) yellow lines on each side.

Question 137 - Road Signs

(B) This is a yield sign, which is the only type of sign that has a downward-pointing triangle shape. When you come to a yield sign, you must slow down and yield to oncoming traffic and pedestrians before proceeding. You may need to stop for them as well, so be prepared.

Question 138 - Road Signs

(B) This out-of-the-ordinary lane control sign indicates that all vehicles in this lane must perform a U-turn. This sign could be accompanied by an equally unusual traffic signal, with lighted U-turn arrows indicating when vehicles can make U-turns.

Question 139 - Road Signs

(C) The road ahead abruptly changes direction. Drivers must reduce their speed to a safe level.

Question 140 - Road Signs

(B) HOV lanes are intended for vehicles that have multiple occupants, such as carpools. This sign indicates that this HOV lane is an HOV 2+ lane, which means that each vehicle must have at least two occupants. That is, there must be a driver and at least one passenger.

Question 141 - Road Signs

(D) This sign serves as a forewarning of an impending yield sign. Be prepared to slow down and yield to vehicles approaching from other directions.

Question 142 - Road Signs

(D) This sign indicates the presence of a shared, central turn lane (also known as a two-way left-turn lane) in the center of the roadway. This lane is designated for left turns (and, where permitted, U-turns) and can be used by vehicles traveling in either direction. A solid yellow line and a broken yellow line mark the lane on each side. This lane must not be used for through traffic at any time. Use caution in this lane because vehicles traveling in the opposite direction may be using it as well.

Question 143 - Road Signs

(C) This sign indicates that there is a low spot ahead on the road. Slow down for your own comfort and control. Proceed with caution and be prepared to stop if the dip becomes flooded.

Question 144 - Road Signs

(C) This sign indicates that the speed limit is 40 miles per hour. This is the fastest you can travel in ideal conditions.

Question 145 - Road Signs

(D) This sign indicates that traffic may flow on both sides of the road.

Question 146 - Road Signs

(D) The main road will curve to the left, with a side road entering from the right, according to this sign. Take extra care when approaching this intersection. A driver preparing to enter the main road from a side road may not notice you approaching from around the curve and may pull out in front of you.

Question 147 - Road Signs

(C) This warning sign indicates that there is a right-hand curve ahead. Just below the sign, a recommended safe speed for the curve may be shown.

Question 148 - Road Signs

(B) This one-way sign warns drivers that they must only travel in the direction indicated by the arrow.

Question 149 - Road Signs
(C) If you see this sign and are traveling slower than the majority of traffic, move to the right lane so that faster traffic can pass you on the left.

Question 150 - Road Signs
(A) This is a wayfinding sign. This sign indicates that food is available

SIGNS AND SITUATIONS

Question 1 - Signs and Situations
(B) This sign warns of a traffic island or other impending hazard. It can be passed on either the left or right side.

Question 2 - Signs and Situations
(C) This sign alerts you that you are approaching an underpass with a vertical clearance of 13'6" (13 feet 6 inches). Trucks can legally be up to 14 feet tall in many Western states (and in a few Western states, even taller).

Question 3 - Signs and Situations
(D) When approaching an intersection controlled by a stop sign, you must come to a complete stop before the stop line. If there is no stop line, you must come to a complete stop before entering a marked or unmarked crosswalk. If there is no crosswalk, you must come to a complete stop before entering the intersection. Yield to oncoming traffic and pedestrians. When it is safe to do so, proceed cautiously through the intersection.

Question 4 - Signs and Situations
(A) When two vehicles arrive at an uncontrolled intersection (one without signs or signals) around the same time, the vehicle on the left must yield to the vehicle on the right. Car A must yield to Car B in this situation.

Question 5 - Signs and Situations
(C) When you can't see well or other drivers can't see you, turn on your headlights. You must use your headlights from half an hour after sunset to half an hour before sunrise, as well as whenever visibility at 500 feet is poor. In addition, unless the wipers are set to intermittent or 'mist', you must use your headlights whenever you use your windshield wipers in bad weather. Your parking lights are intended for parking only, not driving.

Question 6 - Signs and Situations
(A) This is a shared central turning lane with a two-way left turn lane. This lane is for vehicles traveling in either direction making a left turn. Use caution in this lane because vehicles traveling in the opposite direction may be using it as well. This lane should never be used to pass.

Question 7 - Signs and Situations
(A) This pentagonal (five-sided) sign forewarns of an impending school zone or school crossing. Slow down and proceed with caution as school children may be crossing the road ahead. Follow the instructions of the school crossing guards. (Please keep in mind that newer school zones and crossing signs have a fluorescent yellow-green background.)

Question 8 - Signs and Situations

(B) According to the Driver Manual, the following distance of at least two seconds behind the vehicle in front, is recommended. You should increase your following distance even more in hazardous driving conditions.

Question 9 - Signs and Situations
(D) Parking within 15 feet of a fire hydrant is illegal. (There are numerous other places where you are not permitted to park.) Look for any signs or pavement markings that prohibit or limit parking.

Question 10 - Signs and Situations
(A) This sign indicates that there will be a double curve ahead. The road ahead bends to the right, then to the left. (A winding road sign would be posted instead if there was a triple curve ahead.) Slow down, stay to the right and do not pass.

Question 11 - Signs and Situations
(A) A steady yellow traffic light indicates that the light will soon turn red. If it is safe to do so, you should try to stop. (Never try to 'beat the light' by speeding up before it turns red.) But don't come to a sudden halt and risk skidding or being rear-ended by the vehicle in front of you. If you are unable to stop safely, proceed through the intersection with caution.

Question 12 - Signs and Situations
(B) On a green signal, you can turn left after yielding to pedestrians, oncoming vehicles and vehicles already in the intersection.

Question 13 - Signs and Situations
(D) This hand signal is equivalent to the driver's vehicle's brake lights. This driver intends to slow down or come to a complete stop.

Question 14 - Signs and Situations
(A) This sign warns you that traffic from the right lane is about to merge into your lane. Adjust your speed and position to allow merging vehicles to safely merge.

Question 15 - Signs and Situations
(A) Hand signals can be used in place of your vehicle's traditional lighted turn and brake signals. This hand signal indicates a turn to the right.

Question 16 - Signs and Situations
(B) This sign indicates that the divided highway is coming to an end. The road will be converted to a two-way street. Keep to the right and keep an eye out for oncoming traffic.

Question 17 - Signs and Situations
(D) If there is a stop sign, a flashing red signal or a lowered crossing gate at a railroad crossing, you must come to a complete stop. If you must stop, you must do so within 15 to 50 feet of the nearest rail. A railroad crossing gate may not be passed through unless it is completely raised. Always keep an eye out for and listen for approaching trains. warning devices can fail.

Question 18 - Signs and Situations
(D) Before changing lanes, signal and check your mirrors. However, your vehicle has blind spots large enough to conceal another vehicle in the lane next to yours. Motorcyclists are frequently forced to avoid drivers who have failed to check their blind spots. Looking over your shoulder before changing lanes is the only way to check for blind spots. Otherwise, you may fail to notice the vehicle in front of you until it is too late.

Question 19 - Signs and Situations
(A) When two vehicles approach an all-way stop at roughly the same time, the vehicle on the left must yield to the vehicle on the right. Car A must yield to Car B in this situation.

Question 20 - Signs and Situations
(A) If you see a school bus stopped with its red lights flashing on an undivided roadway, you must stop before reaching the bus, whether it is on your side of the road or the opposite side. You must stay stopped until the stop arm retracts and the flashing red lights go out.

Question 21 - Signs and Situations
(B) You must signal continuously for at least the last 100 feet before turning. Even if you don't see any other vehicles, you must signal. The most dangerous vehicle may be one you don't notice.

Question 22 - Signs and Situations

(D) Before proceeding through a red light, you must come to a complete stop and yield to all pedestrians and approaching vehicles.

Question 23 - Signs and Situations
(C) When you come across an emergency vehicle, sanitation vehicle, utility vehicle or wrecker that is stopped with its flashing lights on, you must move into a non-adjacent lane if possible, leaving at least one vacant lane between you and the vehicle. If this is impossible or dangerous (no other lanes in your direction), you must slow down until you have passed the vehicle. The correct slow speeds are listed below. On a four-lane or more-lane highway, you must slow down to 15 mph less than the posted speed limit. On a two-lane highway, you must slow down to 15 mph less than the posted speed limit if it is 25 mph or higher, or 10 mph otherwise. (Note: Although every state in the United States now has its own Move Over Law, some of them require drivers to do different things. Always check the local traffic laws when traveling out of state.)

Question 24 - Signs and Situations
(D) This lane direction sign is a regulatory sign. Vehicles in the left lane must turn left, while vehicles in the right lane may go straight or turn right.

Question 25 - Signs and Situations
(A) A driver turning left at an intersection must first yield to oncoming traffic and crossing

pedestrians. Car A must yield to Car B, who has the right-of-way.

Question 26 - Signs and Situations
(D) In a marked or unmarked crosswalk, a vehicle must yield to pedestrians. In addition, at an uncontrolled intersection (one without signs or signals), each vehicle must yield to the vehicle to its right. As a result, Car A must yield to Car B, who in turn must yield to Car C, who in turn must yield to the pedestrian.

Question 27 - Signs and Situations
(D) This is a yield symbol. Slow down as you approach a yield sign and prepare to yield to pedestrians and traffic ahead. You may need to stop as well, so be prepared.

Question 28 - Signs and Situations
(D) No-Zones are large blind spots on large trucks and buses. In a No-Zone, a car may be completely hidden from the truck driver's view. The truck's side mirrors only provide small arcs of visibility down the sides. A vehicle directly behind or to the side of the truck, just behind the cab, may be in a No-Zone. Car B is currently in one of the truck's No-Zones. It is impossible to always avoid a truck's No-Zones, but don't stay in them for any longer than necessary. Remember that if you can't see the truck driver directly or through one of the truck's mirrors, the truck driver can't see you.

Question 29 - Signs and Situations

(A) Vehicles turning left at an intersection must first yield to oncoming traffic and crossing pedestrians. Car A must yield in this situation.

Question 30 - Signs and Situations
(C) You are not permitted to park within 50 feet of a railroad crossing's nearest rail. (There are numerous other places where you are not permitted to park.) Look for any signs or pavement markings that prohibit or limit parking.

Question 31 - Signs and Situations
(D) When a vehicle hits standing water at a high enough speed, its tyres skip across the water's surface, this is referred to as hydroplaning. Because the tyres will not be in contact with the road, traction will be minimal. At speeds as low as 35 mph, a vehicle can begin to hydroplane. At 55 mph, the tyres may lose contact with the road entirely. A slight turn or even a gust of wind at this point could send the vehicle into an uncontrollable skid. Make sure your tires have enough tread to help prevent hydroplaning. If you come across

Question 32 - Signs and Situations
(D) Hand signals can be used in place of your vehicle's traditional lighted turn and brake signals. This driver intends to make a left turn.

Question 33 - Signs and Situations
(C) You must halt between 15 and 50 feet from the nearest rail when the railroad crossing signals and gates

warn of an approaching train. Use caution and keep an eye on the signals, gates and tracks even after the train has passed, as a second train may arrive soon after the first one. Only until the signals have ceased and the gates have been fully raised may you proceed to cross the tracks.

Question 34 - Signs and Situations
(A) This sign indicates that the maximum speed limit is 50 miles per hour. That is, you are not permitted to exceed 50 mph in this area. Additional signage may be posted to regulate minimum or nighttime speed limits.

Question 35 - Signs and Situations
(C) This sign warns drivers that the road ahead will be divided into a divided highway. A physical barrier, such as a median, will be used to separate opposing lanes. Continue to the right.

Question 36 - Signs and Situations
(B) Unless there is a sign prohibiting it, you may turn left on a red light when turning from one one-way street onto another one-way street. Before turning, you must still come to a complete stop and yield to all pedestrians and traffic. Some states have different laws regarding turning left on red. Always check the local traffic laws when traveling out of state.

Question 37 - Signs and Situations
(A) Turning right on a red light is legal, unless signs are prohibiting it. However, before turning, you must come to a complete stop and yield to pedestrians and traffic.

Question 38 - Signs and Situations
(A) If you're parking on a hill without a curb, point your front wheels toward the road's edge (i.e., away from traffic). If your brakes fail, your car will roll toward the road's edge rather than into traffic. Make certain that your parking brake is still engaged and that your vehicle is in the proper gear. Shift into park, if you have an automatic transmission. When facing downhill, shift into reverse and when facing uphill, shift into first gear for maximum forward torque.

Question 39 - Signs and Situations
(C) Unless signs or pavement markings indicate otherwise, you should cross as few lanes as possible when turning. That is, you should turn left from the left lane and right from the right lane and then into the nearest lane of traffic moving in the right direction. Car A has correctly turned into the closest lane and then merged into the far lane. Car B has made an incorrect turn into the farthest lane.

Question 40 - Signs and Situations
(B) A flashing red signal must be treated as a stop sign. That is, before entering the intersection, you must stop, yield to traffic and pedestrians and then proceed when it is safe to do so.

Question 41 - Signs and Situations

(B) After yielding to all pedestrians and vehicles already in the intersection, you can proceed on a green signal.

Question 42 - Signs and Situations
(C) This sign indicates the presence of a fire station nearby. Keep an eye out for fire trucks as they enter this road.

Question 43 - Signs and Situations
(B) When you have a green signal, you can proceed after yielding to all oncoming traffic and pedestrians in the intersection. Car A should yield to Car B in this situation.

Question 44 - Signs and Situations
(C) If an emergency vehicle with flashing red or blue lights and a siren approaches from either direction, you must proceed through an intersection, pull over to the curb or side of the road and come to a complete stop.

Question 45 - Signs and Situations
(D) This is an advisory sign advising drivers not to exceed 35 mph in this area.

Question 46 - Signs and Situations
(A) You must yield to oncoming traffic before turning left into an alley or driveway. And, whenever you drive into or out of a driveway or alley, you must come to a complete stop before crossing the sidewalk and yield to pedestrians

Question 47 - Signs and Situations

(B) When parallel parking facing uphill, turn your wheels away from the curb and then roll back slightly so that the back part of the curbside front wheel rests against the curb. The curb will prevent your car from rolling backward if your brakes fail. Make certain that your parking brake is still engaged and that your vehicle is in the proper gear (Park for an automatic transmission or first gear for maximum forward torque, with a manual transmission).

Question 48 - Signs and Situations
(B) When you are within 500 feet of an oncoming vehicle or within 200 feet of a vehicle you are following, you must dim your high beams. Avoid shining your high beams on any other vehicle that is occupied. If you dim your high beams before they shine on other vehicles, those other drivers may reciprocate.

Question 49 - Signs and Situations
(A) When you come to a complete stop at a stop sign, you must do so before the stop line, crosswalk or intersection, whichever comes first. After that, yield to pedestrians and other vehicles and proceed only when the intersection is clear.

Question 50 - Signs and Situations
(D) You must always obey a police officer or a firefighter's instructions, even if it means disregarding other traffic devices or rules. For example, if a police officer waves you through a red light or a stop sign, you should proceed.

FINE & LIMITS

Question 1 - Fines & Limits

(C) A learner's license holder under the age of 18 must complete numerous prerequisites before being given a driver license. For one, a parent, guardian, or responsible adult 21 or older must verify that the learner driver has completed at least 50 hours of driving experience, including 10 hours at night. [Class E Driver License Requirements, 10. Obtaining Your License or ID Card, Official Florida Driver's Handbook]

Question 2 - Fines & Limits

(C) The Class E driver license is intended for non-commercial vehicle operators. Commercial driver licenses are classified into three classes: A, B, and C. (CDLs). [Florida Driver License Classification, Official Florida Driver's Handbook, 10. Obtaining Your License or ID Card]

Question 3 - Fines & Limits

(D) While you have a learner's permit, you must drive under the supervision of a licensed driver who is at least 21 years old and seated next to you in the front seat. [From the Official Florida Driver's Handbook, Important Information for Minor Drivers]

Question 4 - Fines & Limits

(B) If you are found guilty of at least three major offenses or fifteen pointable offenses within five years, you will be designated as a Habitual Traffic Offender (HTO) and your license will be terminated. DUI, vehicular manslaughter, driving while your license is suspended or revoked, and leaving the scene of an accident in which someone was hurt or killed are all serious charges. [Losing Your Driving Privilege, 9. Your Driving Privilege, Official Florida Driver's Handbook], [FL Stat 322]. .264]

Question 5 - Fines & Limits

(C) A Class E driver license can only be obtained if you are at least 16 years old. [Class E Driver License Requirements, 10. Obtaining Your License or ID Card, Official Florida Driver's Handbook]

Question 6 - Fines & Limits

(D) Under certain conditions, Florida's Financial Responsibility Law mandates you to purchase Bodily Injury Liability (BIL) coverage in addition to the standard Personal Injury Protection (PIP) and Property Damage Liability (PDL) coverage on your car. These scenarios include being convicted of DUI, having your license suspended for accumulating too many points, causing an accident in which someone was harmed, or having your license revoked for committing too many major traffic violations. [Insurance Laws, 9. Your Driving Privilege, Florida Driver's Handbook]

Question 7 - Fines & Limits

(B) If you acquire 24 points in 36 months, your license will be suspended for up to a year. [9. Your Driving Privilege, Official Florida Driver's Handbook, Point System]

Question 8 - Fines & Limits

(D) If you are obliged by Florida law to obtain Bodily Injury Liability (BIL) insurance coverage for your car but fail to do so, your driver license, vehicle license plates, or both may be suspended for up to three years. You could also be fined up to $500, imprisoned for up to 60 days, or both. [Insurance Laws, 9. Your Driving Privilege, Official Florida Driver's Handbook], [FL Statutes 324.023], [FL Statutes 324.221], [FL Statutes 775.082], [FL Statutes 775]. .083]

Question 9 - Fines & Limits

(D) If you are convicted of DUI for the third time, you will face the following penalties: a $2,000 – $5,000 fine, up to one year in jail, license revocation for at least 180 days, and 21 hours of DUI school. For at least two years, you will also be required to install an ignition interlock device (IID) in each motor vehicle you possess. If your blood alcohol level (BAL) exceeds a predetermined limit, the IID will prevent your vehicle from starting. If you had a passenger under the age of 18 in your car at the time of the incident or your BAL was 0.15 percent or higher, the fine will range between $4,000 and $5,000. [Penalties for DUI, 9. Your Driving Privilege, Official Florida Driver's Handbook]

Question 10 - Fines & Limits

(D) The hours that a driver under the age of 18 may drive unaccompanied are limited. If an underage driver is found to be in violation of these rules, three points will be added to his or her driving record. In Florida, three points is the smallest number of points for any pointable traffic offence. [9. Your Driving Privilege, Official Florida Driver's Handbook, Point System]

DISTRACTED DRIVING

Question 1 - Distracted Driving
(D) You should also be cautious of the following potential distractions and impairments: 1) Alcohol, narcotics and even some prescriptions can impair your ability to drive. 2) Listening to overly loud music or utilizing technologies such as cell phones, GPS and intercoms while driving can also impair your concentration. 3) Adjusting your vehicle's technological controls and features can be distracting and quickly impair your ability to scan for and react to risks. 4) Emotional and physical states such as exhaustion, rage, illness, worry and terror can all impact your driving abilities.

Question 2 - Distracted Driving
(D) When you are driving, read the label before taking a drug to see if there are any precautions about its side effects. If you are unsure if it is safe to take the medication and drive, consult your doctor or pharmacist about any potential adverse effects. Drugs used to treat headaches, colds, hay fever or other allergies or to calm nerves might make a person drowsy and impair driving ability. Other prescription medicines ingredients, like alcohol, can impair your reflexes, judgment, eyesight and awareness.

Question 3 - Distracted Driving
(B) Turning around to attend to the needs of passengers, children or pets should not distract your attention away from the road. If you need to tend to passengers or animals, pull over to the side of the road and park.

Question 4 - Distracted Driving
(B) Before you begin your journey, you should customize your cab to your liking, however eating and drinking should be done at rest stops.

Question 5 - Distracted Driving
(D) Stimulants, exercise and music can help you stay awake, but the greatest solution for drowsiness is sleep. Consult a doctor if you're getting 9 hours of sleep but still feeling fatigued.

Question 6 - Distracted Driving
(D) The monotony of the road and traffic, the buzz of the wind, tires and engine noise all contribute to highway hypnosis or dizziness when driving. Drivers can avoid highway hypnosis by shifting their eyes regularly and paying attention to the traffic and highway signs around them.

Question 7 - Distracted Driving
(A) Driving while using a visual screen device or texting is illegal. Acting in this manner while driving is against the law.

Question 8 - Distracted Driving
(C) Cell phones are not permitted to be used by underage drivers while driving unless to notify an emergency.

Question 9 - Distracted Driving

(B) Even on a straightaway or an empty road, a distraction is still a distraction. While driving, do not eat, drink, smoke, text, read or engage in unpleasant conversation. If at all feasible, turn off your phone and leave it turned off until you are finished driving for the day.

Question 10 - Distracted Driving

(D) Texting or eating while driving raises your chances of being involved in an accident. If you get lost, pull over and enter navigation directions. You can, however, utilize audio navigation while driving.

Question 11 - Distracted Driving

(D) Many prescription and over-the-counter drugs have the potential to make you drowsy. Take drugs while driving only if your doctor says they won't impair your ability to drive safely.

Question 12 - Distracted Driving

(D) Talking on a cell phone while driving increases your chances of being in a crash by up to four times. This is because the talk is diverting your focus away from your driving. Sending text messages (texting) while driving increases your chances of getting involved in an accident by up to eight times.

Question 13 - Distracted Driving

(A) Any activity that takes your eyes off the road while driving, such as removing clothing, doing makeup, reading, eating or drinking, is risky.

Do not carry someone, a pet or a package in your lap or arms.

Question 14 - Distracted Driving

(A) Anything that takes your attention away from the road can cause you to become distracted. Texting, talking on the phone, dealing with children and lighting a cigarette are all examples of distractions while driving.

Question 15 - Distracted Driving

(A) Texting and driving is currently the biggest cause of death among teenagers, accounting for 25% of all car accidents in the United States. It is against the law to send text texts while driving.

Question 16 - Distracted Driving

(D) Prescription drugs, illegal narcotics and over-the-counter medications can all impair your ability to drive safely.

Question 17 - Distracted Driving

(B) If you are an adult driver and really must use your phone while driving, utilize a speakerphone/hands-free device. Using a cell phone while driving is not encouraged and is even illegal in some places.

Question 18 - Distracted Driving

(C) It is illegal for a minor to drive while using a cell phone. If his or her cell phone rings, he or she should not answer it. Violations of this law are punishable by fines.

Question 19 - Distracted Driving

(D) Fatigue can impair your judgment, lower your reaction times and reduce your awareness of your surroundings when driving.

Question 20 - Distracted Driving
(A) Any activity that requires you to use your hands while driving should be avoided. Listening to the radio, on the other hand, can assist you in remaining alert.

DRINKING AND DRIVING

Question 1 - Drinking and Driving
(D) It is illegal for a minor between the ages of fifteen and twenty-one to be in the possession of alcohol, consume alcohol, attempt to purchase or purchase alcohol, or have a blood alcohol concentration (BAC) of 0.02 percent or higher.

Question 2 - Drinking and Driving
(D) All of the responses have the same quantity of alcohol.

Question 3 - Drinking and Driving
(A) The presence of open containers of alcohol in any area within reach of the vehicle's driver or passenger is prohibited by the Open Container Law. Limousines, taxis, motor homes and commercial buses are exempt.

Question 4 - Drinking and Driving
(D) Alcohol can impair your concentration, reaction time and decision-making abilities.

Question 5 - Drinking and Driving
(A) According to the National Safety Council, someone dies in an alcohol-related crash every 33 minutes. Drunk driving is the leading single cause of death in young people aged 16 to 24. According to statistics, 112 million US drivers drank too much and went behind the wheel in 2010.

Question 6 - Drinking and Driving
(D) Your blood alcohol content is affected by how quickly you drink, how many drinks you've had and how much you weigh (BAC).

Question 7 - Drinking and Driving
(D) Regardless of the form, one drink typically contains a one and a half ounce serving of alcohol.

Question 8 - Drinking and Driving
(B) Drinking alcohol and driving at night is extremely risky because your vision is already limited due to the darkness and difficulty of seeing.

Question 9 - Drinking and Driving
(D) A drunk driver is more prone to drive too fast or too slowly, to change lanes repeatedly and to fail to dim the headlights. Even more importantly, in an emergency, an intoxicated driver may be less aware and may take too long to brake. Such errors may jeopardize both the driver and others.

Question 10 - Drinking and Driving
(D) When you consume alcohol, it enters your system and begins to influence all of your bodily processes, including coordination, self-control and reaction time. The only 'cure' for alcohol's effects on the brain is to wait for it to leave your system.

Question 11 - Drinking and Driving
(A) Only time can clear alcohol from one's system. People wrongly believe that coffee and fresh air will conceal the effects of alcohol, such

as tiredness and slowed reactions, but they will not change the fact that you will be driving under the influence until a sufficient amount of time has passed after drinking.

Question 12 - Drinking and Driving
(A) By operating a motor vehicle, you have consented to submit to a chemical test if asked by a police officer if you are arrested for driving under the influence of intoxicants.

Question 13 - Drinking and Driving
(D) Open containers of alcohol may only be stored in areas where drivers and passengers cannot reach them, such as cargo areas, trunks and truck beds.

Question 14 - Drinking and Driving
(D) Alcohol can impair vision, slow reaction times and dull judgment. Alcohol has no effect on alertness.

Question 15 - Drinking and Driving
(D) Alcohol use before or while driving impairs reflexes, physical control of a vehicle and awareness of potential hazards on the road.

Question 16 - Drinking and Driving
(D) If you intend to drink alcohol, you should also plan to use public transportation, a taxi or arrange a designated driver to go home.

Question 17 - Drinking and Driving
(D) If you are convicted of driving under the influence of alcohol or drugs, you could face license suspension, steep fines and community service.

Question 18 - Drinking and Driving
(D) Unless you are 21 years old, you are not permitted to purchase, drink or possess alcohol.

Question 19 - Drinking and Driving
(B) The amount of alcohol that each person can consume before exceeding the legal limit varies from person to person and is determined by a number of factors.

Question 20 - Drinking and Driving
(D) Even a modest amount of alcohol can impair a driver's reflexes, driving ability and depth perception.

Question 21 - Drinking and Driving
(B) The type of alcohol has no effect on the blood alcohol content. Each type of alcohol has the same amount in a standard serving.

Question 22 - Drinking and Driving
(D) Your driver's license will be suspended if you are a juvenile and are convicted of driving under the influence of drugs or transporting an open container of any alcoholic beverage.

Question 23 - Drinking and Driving
(C) The more alcohol that enters your body to intoxicate you, the longer it will take your liver to break it down. One normal drink (one ounce of hard liquor, one-half glass of wine or a 12-ounce can of beer) can be broken down by the liver in roughly an hour. If you drink a lot of

alcohol, it can take up to a day or two for your body to fully recover.

Question 24 - Drinking and Driving
(A) To drive your vehicle, you must nominate a designated driver. The designated driver is in charge of transporting friends or family members, who have consumed alcoholic beverages, safely.

Question 25 - Drinking and Driving
(A) If you refuse to submit to the requisite blood and/or urine test(s), your driving privileges may be revoked.

EXAM TEST PRACTICE

.

Question 1 - Mock Exam

(A) Work zone signs are often orange in color. Yellow or fluorescent yellow-green warning signs are used permanently.

Question 2 - Mock Exam

(C) This is a yield sign, which is the only form of sign that has a downward-pointing triangle shape. When you come to a yield sign, you must slow down and surrender to oncoming traffic and pedestrians before proceeding. You may need to stop for them as well, so be prepared.

Question 3 - Mock Exam

(D) Exit ramps allow cars to slow down and exit highways. At an exit ramp, a lower speed is frequently posted.

Question 4 - Mock Exam

(D) In Florida, if an emergency vehicle approaches you in a roundabout with a siren or flashing lights, continue to the nearest exit, then pull over and let the emergency vehicle pass. ["Florida Roundabouts: Frequently Asked Questions," Florida Department of Transportation, https://www.fdot.gov/agencyreso urces/roundabouts/faq.html] .shtm]

Question 5 - Mock Exam

(D) When passing another vehicle, try to get through the other driver's blind spot as rapidly as possible while staying under the speed limit. The longer you stay in the blind region, the more likely it is that you will collide. When passing, you must not exceed the speed limit.

Question 6 - Mock Exam

(D) Don't stop, back up, or try to turn around if you miss your exit on a limited-access highway. This dramatically increases the possibility of a collision. Backing up on a limited-access highway is banned in Florida. Instead, proceed to the next exit and find a method to return from there.

Question 7 - Mock Exam

(A) On one-way and divided highways, solid yellow lines are used as left-edge lines.

Question 8 - Mock Exam

(A) "At an open (uncontrolled) T-intersection, the vehicle on the through route must yield to cars on the terminating road," is FALSE. At an open T-intersection, the vehicle on the terminating road must yield to cars on the through route.

Question 9 - Mock Exam

(D) A no-passing zone is denoted by a solid yellow line. If there is a solid yellow line adjacent to your lane, you are not permitted to pass. It's also against the law to drive past a halted school bus with flashing red lights. Also, do not pass when approaching a hill or curve when vision is limited.

Question 10 - Mock Exam

(D) If your rear wheels begin to skid, DON'T PANIC and STOP YET. Instead, turn the steering wheel in the desired direction of your car. If your rear wheels are sliding to the left, steer to the left; if they are sliding to the right, steer to the right. The rear wheels may overshoot and begin skidding in the opposite direction. To avoid this, move the steering wheel in the opposite direction as soon as your car begins to straighten out. This approach, known as "steering into the skid," will bring your vehicle's rear into level with the front.

Question 11 - Mock Exam

(B) The brakes will fade if you continue to apply them to regulate your speed on a steep downhill (lose their effectiveness). Instead, let go of the gas and move into a lower gear (even with an automatic transmission). This will produce a braking effect, known as engine braking, to slow the car. The stronger the engine braking impact, the lower the gear. Only use the brakes when engine braking is insufficient or you wish to come to a complete stop.

Question 12 - Mock Exam

(B) A red circle and slash on a prohibitory sign means "no." This

sign indicates that left turns are not permitted in this area.

Question 13 - Mock Exam

(B) When turning left from a two-way street onto a one-way street, start with your left wheel as close to the yellow dividing line as possible.

Question 14 - Mock Exam

(A) On a wet road, modern tires will normally channel water away to keep contact with the road at speeds of up to 35 mph. However, at higher speeds in deep water, the tire's channeling motion becomes less effective, and the tires begin to ride on a layer of water like water skis. This is known as "hydroplaning." At speeds of 50 mph or higher, hydroplaning can cause a complete loss of braking and steering control. To avoid hydroplaning, make sure your tires have enough tread, that they are properly inflated, and that you drive slowly. In wet weather, always increase your following distance.

Question 15 - Mock Exam

(C) When the sun is shining brightly or when a line of vehicles behind you may hide your turn signal light, utilize hand signals. Hand signals, on the other hand, may not be visible at night unless in well-lit regions.

Question 16 - Mock Exam

(A) If you're going quicker than the rest of the traffic on an expressway, stay in the center or left lane.

Vehicles that go at a slower speed should use the right lane.

Question 17 - Mock Exam

(A) A blind or visually challenged pedestrian is one who uses a white cane or a guide dog. You should always give such pedestrians the right-of-way. If a pedestrian with a white cane or a guiding dog is preparing to cross the road in front of you, you must come to a complete stop and cede the right-of-way to the pedestrian, according to Florida law. Don't honk your horn since it may frighten a pedestrian or a guide dog. [Florida Statute 316] .1301]

Question 18 - Mock Exam

(A) Slow down and encourage the motorist behind you to pass if you are being tailgated. If this fails, pull over, come to a complete stop, and allow the tailgater pass. Don't try to outrun or outpace the tailgater by increasing your speed. Some tailgaters believe that no speed is too fast.

Question 19 - Mock Exam

(C) If you can't make a U-turn because the route is too narrow, you can turn around by making a three-point turn. This move will also send you in the other direction. You should only make a three-point turn if visibility is good, traffic is light on both sides of the road, the turn is permitted, and there is no other way to turn around.

Question 20 - Mock Exam

(A) When you see a flashing yellow light, you should slow down and proceed with caution. Flashing yellow lights are placed in potentially hazardous areas.

Question 21 - Mock Exam

(A) Before you back up, be sure it's safe to do so and that it won't interfere with oncoming traffic. It is a good idea to stroll behind the vehicle to ensure that there is no child, pet, or toy in the path. Turn your head to see over your shoulder and through the back window. You should not rely on your mirrors because they have blind zones.

Question 22 - Mock Exam

(A) Signs for construction, maintenance, or emergency operations are usually rectangular or diamond-shaped, with black characters or symbols on an orange background. They serve as a warning to drivers that construction is taking place on or near the route.

Question 23 - Mock Exam

(A) This sign warns that there will be a roundabout ahead. A roundabout is a circular crossroads with traffic flowing counterclockwise around a central island. Slow down and prepare to yield to oncoming traffic on the roundabout.

Question 24 - Mock Exam

(A) Bicyclists can be difficult to notice on the road, so keep an eye out for them. Slow down and check for oncoming traffic before passing a bicycle traveling in your way. When passing a bicycle, you must provide at least three feet of space between your vehicle and the bicycle, according to Florida law.

Question 25 - Mock Exam

(D) In Florida, you must have a placard or a special license plate for disabled people or disabled veterans to park in a blue parking place.

Question 26 - Mock Exam

(D) When there are no approaching vehicles, on unknown roads, in construction zones, or where there may be people alongside the road you are going on, use your high-beam headlights.

Question 27 - Mock Exam

(B) A solid white line marks the freeway's outer boundary in either direction. Following that comes the shoulder, which should only be utilized in an emergency. Never drive or pass on the shoulder of the road.

Question 28 - Mock Exam

(D) Highway hypnosis is a state of tiredness or unawareness caused by boredom, the sounds of the wind and tyres on the road, and the constant hum of the motor. Avoid the condition by moving your gaze from one side of the road to the other and concentrate on various items close and far, left and right. Talking on a cell phone or often changing lanes might be hazardous.

Question 29 - Mock Exam

(C) Some illegal drugs, prescription pharmaceuticals, and over-the-counter medications can produce drowsiness, sleepiness, or decreased coordination, which can impair your ability to drive. If you are unsure about the side effects of a medicine, consult the warning label or your pharmacist or doctor.

Question 30 - Mock Exam

(D) While waiting for approaching traffic to clear before making a left turn, keep your front wheels pointed straight ahead until the turn begins. If another car hits you from behind, this will prevent you from being forced into oncoming traffic.

Question 31 - Mock Exam

(C) This is a No-Entry sign. It signifies that you are not permitted to access the road where the sign is located. Such signs will be found at road openings that you should not enter or where you would be going the wrong way on a one-way street. These signs can be found at exit ramps, at crossovers on split highways, and in a variety of locations on one-way streets.

Question 32 - Mock Exam

(D) Road rage is demonstrated by cutting off or swerving in front of other vehicles. Excessive horn use, forcing a car off the road, and tailgating are all symptoms of road rage.

Question 33 - Mock Exam

(B) Make it clear to other drivers what your goals are. Continue to signal until you are ready to make the turn. Extending the hand and arm outward is the proper hand gesture for making a left turn.

Question 34 - Mock Exam

(D) When feasible, maintain the same approximate speed as other vehicles, but never exceed the posted speed restrictions. Stay in the lane closest to the right side of the road if you are traveling slower than other vehicles.

Question 35 - Mock Exam

(B) Head restraints are intended to protect your neck if you are assaulted from behind. Headrests should be positioned so that in the event of an accident, the head restraint contacts the back of the head.

Question 36 - Mock Exam

(D) Mile markers (also known as mileposts) are placed along the outside shoulder of the highway to mark the edge of the road and provide drivers with information about their location on the highway for navigation and emergency purposes. Exit numbers on Florida's interstate highways correspond to mile markers along the route.

Question 37 - Mock Exam

(D) When leaving a parallel parking place, check over your shoulder as well as in your mirrors. Then, before entering traffic, wait until the road is clear. You should signal your intention, enter traffic in the adjacent lane, and stay in that lane until it is safe to change to another lane.

Question 38 - Mock Exam

(D) If you are one of the first people to arrive at a collision scene, the first thing you should do is pull your vehicle off the road. If there is no danger of fire, do not transfer injured people. Notify emergency personnel and avoid standing in traffic lanes. Inquire of those who have stopped to warn oncoming traffic.

Question 39 - Mock Exam

(D) When there is a solid and a broken yellow line between opposing lanes of traffic, you may pass if the broken yellow line is on your side but not if the solid yellow line is on your side.

Question 40 - Mock Exam

(D) The divided highway terminates 350 to 500 feet ahead, according to this notice. The road will be converted to a two-way street. Keep to the right and keep an eye out for oncoming traffic.

Question 41 - Mock Exam

(D) Unless otherwise indicated by signs or signals, you must begin your left turn in the leftmost lane.

Question 42 - Mock Exam

(C) Parking places for people with disabilities are denoted by blue pavement markers.

Question 43 - Mock Exam

(B) You are not compelled to turn into the lane that is the furthest from where you came from, whether you are turning right or left. When performing a right turn, you must enter the lane nearest to where you came from. The restrictions for making a left turn onto a multilane highway in Florida differ from those in other states. When turning left in Florida, you are not required to enter the nearest lane that is traveling in the correct direction. You may turn left into any lane that is legally open and safe for you to do so. [Making Turns; 5. Driving Safely; Florida Driver License Handbook], [FL Stat § 316.151]

Question 44 - Mock Exam

(B) A two-way left-turn lane (also known as a shared center turn lane) is designated for making left turns (and, where authorized, U-turns) and can be utilized by cars driving in either direction. A solid yellow line and a broken yellow line mark the lane on each side. This lane should never be utilized for passing or cutting through traffic. Use caution in this lane because vehicles heading in the opposite direction may be using it as well.

Question 45 - Mock Exam

(B) You have blind zones no matter what kind of vehicle you drive or how you adjust your mirrors. There are blind spots in every vehicle. The most prevalent blind spots are found in the vehicle's left and right rear corners. In general, the larger the vehicle, the more blind spots there are. No-Zones are enormous blind zones on trucks.

Question 46 - Mock Exam

(D) When there is standing water on a roadway, hydroplaning happens. Most tires will channel water away from the vehicle at speeds up to 35 mph, similar to how a windshield wiper cleans the windshield. As your speed grows, the tires' ability to channel water decreases, and your tires may lose touch with the road and ride over the water like a pair of water skis. Partially hydroplaning can occur in a common passenger car at speeds as low as 35 mph.

Question 47 - Mock Exam

(A) Do not obstruct a junction. You must proceed if you have already entered the junction when the green light or green arrow turns yellow or red. Clear the junction by performing the motion you planned.

Question 48 - Mock Exam

(B) The brakes will fade if you continue to apply them to regulate your speed on a steep downhill (lose their effectiveness). Instead, let go of the gas and move into a lower gear (even with an automatic transmission). This will produce a braking effect, known as engine braking, to slow the car. The stronger the engine braking impact, the lower the gear. Only use the brakes when engine braking is insufficient or you wish to come to a complete stop.

Question 49 - Mock Exam

(D) If an emergency vehicle approaches you with its siren and flashing lights activated, you must go clear of any intersection, yield to the emergency vehicle, pull over to the nearest edge of the roadway, and remain stopped until the emergency vehicle has passed. [Florida Statute 316] .126]

Question 50 - Mock Exam

(B) When turning left at a controlled intersection (one that has signs or signals), you must first yield to oncoming cars and pedestrians within the crosswalk or intersection.

A MESSAGE FROM THE DRIVING SCHOOL

First and foremost, we want to thank you for choosing this book. We hope it has, in some manner, added value to your life.

If you enjoyed this book and found the practice tests useful, please let us know. We would greatly appreciate if you could post a review on Amazon.

Your feedback and support will be invaluable in assisting us, to improve our next books and make the current one even better.

Thank you so much,

The Driving School

Made in United States
Orlando, FL
29 May 2025